T5-AGP-881

SINUS TONE PRODUCTION

By the Same Author

Light on the Voice Beautiful
Science and Singing
Formerly 'The Voice Beautiful'
Vocal Exercises
Chart for Vocal Exercises, etc.

'MUMMY, WHY DOES SHE SCREAM WHEN SHE YAWNS?'

Reproduced by kind permission of the Proprietors of 'Punch'

The correct position of the throat will be experienced during a yawn or an attempted yawn.—*No Need to Stammer*, by H. ST. JOHN RUMSEY.

SINUS TONE PRODUCTION

BY

ERNEST G. WHITE

WITH 21 PHOTOGRAPHS AND DIAGRAMS

CRESCENDO PUBLISHING COMPANY
Boston

Standard Book Number 87597-036-2
Library of Congress Card Number 74-109155
Printed in the United States of America
Reprinted by arrangement with
J. M. Dent & Sons Ltd., London
holders of the copyright.

Affectionately Inscribed

To MY WIFE

WHOSE LOVING CARE HAS HELPED ME

THROUGH MANY DIFFICULTIES

FOREWORD

It must not be assumed that because my profession happens to be music that it is to musicians only, nor even to musicians first, that I would commend this book. It should be remembered that vocalism is ' the use of the voice in speaking or singing ' and in that sense we are all therefore, with few sad exceptions*, vocalists.

To the artist I would quote especially :—

> " I like too Mr. White's insistence on the necessity for mechanical control prior to poetical freedom : it is a truth basic to all art, to all poetry."—(*Dr. Oliver C-de-C. Ellis*)

And to those whose aim in studying S.T.P. is not an artistic one, but some other, I would specially cite :—

> " The worse the condition of the voice the more it needs training . . . for health reasons "—(*Chapter II, p. 28*)

During the years that have passed since the publication of the first edition of this book, the knowledge of Ernest G. White's discoveries has spread and the number of those putting the theory to practical use is very greatly increased. This result has not been brought about by a widespread advertising campaign, but is the snowball-like growth inevitably resulting from propagation of truth.

That the whole may not have been laid bare by his premises White himself realized—" no claim is made as to finality " (p.2)—and Dr. Ellis in his Introduction to the book in 1938 said " There may be some things in this book with which the reader will not agree . . . but he should not allow them to interfere with his consideration of the main thesis of the book." Twelve years later we can say that nothing has happened disproving that ' main thesis of the book ', and from the constantly accumulating evidence of the benefits resulting from the application of White's principles—in the art fields of speech and music certainly, but also in the wider sphere of physical health—it is made manifest

**It is not too much to say that the number of sad exceptions will be reduced with the proper application of Sinus Tone principles.*

that a seeker after truth cannot afford to ignore " Sinus Tone Production ".

This accumulation of evidence continues to show that whatever in the way of voice, may be the best of which an individual human machine is capable, that will S.T.P. find for him and show to him. And the most recent evidence would seem to prove that in all cases where difficulty is experienced in discovering or developing a beautiful voice, the cause is always either a malformation or some trouble only indirectly concerned with the vocal machine, but which, necessarily, must affect its work. (For it is not a matter of contention that " if one member suffer all the members suffer with it ; though this may not always appear to be the case.) Indeed when one sits quietly back and recognizes that the instrument called ' voice ' consists merely of certain parts of the machine called ' body ', and is *NOT* in fact, a thing complete in itself at all, then it appears clearly the most natural thing on earth that its health and well-being, its proper behaviour, its fitness to do all that is required of it and all that is *possible* to it, must in part depend on the well-being and functional relationship of all the other parts of the same body.

If at first sight this statement appears to weaken the case for S.T.P. I beg the reader to reflect : Ernest White never claimed for his discoveries more than that they were the elucidation of the truth about (i) how voice is produced and controlled and (ii) what, in fact, was the function of the vocal cords. Those of us who, since E. G. W's death in 1940 have tried to keep his memory green and carry his work forward to its next stage need for the purpose no better or higher aim.

RONALD DUSSEK

1950

PREFACE

> Man's province is work : his day is a battle against obstacles. . . . The joy of labour, the joy of giving are the wages of God.—J. K. JEROME.

THIS volume completes the series of three in which I have set down my discoveries on the subject of the voice, and explained as clearly as I am able the principles of Sinus Tone Production. Until I published my first book, under the title of *Science and Singing*, in 1909, no one, I believe, had assigned to the cranial sinuses any place of utility in our natural economy, nor even given them any serious thought. In that book I propounded my thesis that these sinuses are the seat of vocal tone production, and gave an account of the researches which had led me to that conclusion. In my second book, *Light on the Voice Beautiful*, I recapitulated and replied to the controversies which this conclusion had aroused. This final volume gives a fuller elucidation than has hitherto been possible of the theories which govern the Sinus Tone Production method ; and further explains what is the exact procedure which will ensure the development of beautiful vocal tone.

' Man's day is a battle against obstacles.' Surely few men have experienced so many obstacles in proclaiming a new truth as the author of this book. His whole life has been spent in overcoming them, and now having passed the age of threescore years and ten, he can look back and endorse the idea that to have a definite mission in life brings a ' joy of labour ' and constitutes the ' wages of God.' Carlyle was not far wrong when he said, ' Blessed is he who has found his work ; let him ask no other blessedness.' This, with the ' joy of giving ' health, strength and renewed vitality to the sick, is the only wages I have received for life's battle against obstacles. And as they undoubtedly constitute the most valuable wages which one can receive, perhaps contentment should fill the mind.

It is, however, a frailty of human nature, to which I must plead guilty, to look for—if not to sigh for—some definite recognition at the hands of those overlords of orthodoxy who bear rule in that particular department of life in which one's work has been accomplished. 'Justice,' it has been said, 'travels with leaden foot, but strikes with an iron hand.' The leaden foot I have certainly experienced, but the iron hand has not yet reformed the vocalist's kingdom. If I may liken that kingdom to a certain Jericho, moated, fortified and strongly walled by the established method of orthodoxy, I would say that I have blown a vigorous trumpet blast before its walls, and although the walls have not yet fallen flat, some obvious rents and fractures have been made which show a weakening in the city's defence. A few more blasts and the rulers of this Jericho will be forced to admit defeat.

That is a prediction for the future ; in the meantime it is more profitable to study the present.

The science of Sinus Tone Production is 'a new playground for thought. Let us play in it a little in order to familiarize ourselves with it.' The following pages are written primarily for those who, having already accepted the theory of Sinus Tone Production, wish to familiarize themselves with its details and its importance. I have thought it advisable to carry out the plan suggested by Ernest Newman, namely, that a right theory of any subject can be established only by destructive criticism in the first place of any wrong theory that happens to hold the field at the moment. In the first chapter, therefore, I enumerate some of the contradictions and absurdities to be found in the vocal cord theory of voice, followed by an explanation of Sinus theories in Chapter II. Chapters III and IV deal chiefly with medical matters, and Chapter V with the artistic side.

I hope that this arrangement may also help another group of readers, who may have to approach this book in the spirit of Michael Faraday. Of him it has been said that he was 'capable of working hopefully in fields from which the well-schooled man of science expected nothing.' Such is, or used to be, the position concerning the utility of the cranial sinuses. Until 1909 the vocalist was unaware that he possessed any, and therefore he could expect nothing from them ; and medical men seeing that they had no muscular or obvious connection with any other part of the human system left them severely alone. It was not until after I lost my voice, both speaking and singing, in my so-called training, that I discovered even that sinuses formed a part of our anatomy, and then followed years of thought and research as to their possible utility. I spent years in the endeavour to prove by mechanical means that the vocal cords cannot produce tone. By my own direction experiments were carried out on my person which were so trying in their effect that I was given restoratives at the conclusion of one or two of these attempts. Eventually the proof came from logic, put to a practical test with a triumphant result. 'The proper and only question to ask concerning a scientific hypothesis,' says Montague Slater, 'is, "Does it work?" not "Is it true?" but science became so proud she asked the wrong question.' The formulae for Sinus teaching were fermenting in my mind for a long time while the question 'Is it true?' was continually uppermost. At length came the opportunity for a crucial test, 'Does it work?' and the affirmative answer was given in a manner which precluded all doubt. This book offers further evidence on the same lines, and is offered to the public in the earnest hope that it will spread the truth and benefits of Sinus Tone Production still further and wider.

E. G. W.

1938.

ACKNOWLEDGEMENTS

My special thanks are due to Mr. Arthur D. Hewlett who, in addition to his enthusiasm in making known the principles of Sinus Tone Production, spent much time and care in revising the order of the material in this Manuscript. My thanks are also due to the editor of *Musical Opinion* for putting at my disposal a considerable amount of space in his columns for the discussion of Sinus Theories of voice.

The frontispiece is taken from *Punch*, with the permission of the Proprietors. Figure 1 is reproduced from the original in the British Museum by the courtesy of the authorities of the Print Room and with the permission of the Director; Figures 3 and 4 are from photographs by Dr. Isaac Roberts, F.R.S. and Figures 9 and 10 from Werner Spateholz's *Hand Atlas of Human Anatomy* by permission of Herr S. Hirzel. Figure 11 is reproduced from *Cunningham's Textbook of Anatomy* by kind permission of the Oxford University Press; Figure 13 was very kindly drawn for me by my pupil, the Rev. Sylvester Fryer, O.S.B., of Ampleforth Abbey; and Figures 14-20 are taken, with permission, from Dr. Pettigrew's *Design in Nature*, published by Longmans, Green & Co.

I am grateful to many publishers and authors for permission to quote extracts from their works; reference is made at the point of the book in which quotations are printed.

E. G. W.

CONTENTS

ILLUSTRATIONS

CHAPTER I

THE TRUTH OF SINUS TONE PRODUCTION

Read not to Contradict and Confute; nor to Beleeve and Take for Granted; Nor to Finde Talke and Discourse; But to Weigh and Consider.—FRANCIS BACON.

'THERE is quite as much fun, and perhaps as much sense, in pursuing a fact as in pursuing a fox; and whereas not even those who hunt the fox love him for his own sake, it *is* possible to love truth for its own sake even in the act of tracking it down remorselessly.' So pleasantly writes Ernest Newman in his Foreword to that excellent and entertaining book, *Fact and Fiction about Wagner.*[1] Continuing on another page he says: 'In the present volume I have tried to give the reader some indication of the immense amount of painful research work that is often necessary before a single disputable fact can be established, or a truth the size of a pin's head can be substituted for a legend that has grown and grown till at last it is the size of a mountain.'

It was nearly forty years ago that I started in the pursuit of an idea which I hoped would eventually prove to be a truth. The burden of the idea was the inability of the vocal cords to produce voice. For the whole of that time I have been 'tracking it down remorselessly,' both on account of the love of truth, and also on account of what I conceived would be the value of the truth.

The legend of vocal cord values, which has never been anything more than a tradition, has during the 1,700 years of its existence grown indeed to 'the size of a mountain,' on which the élite of medical, scientific and musical pedagogues love to disport and air themselves. If, as Mr. Newman says, it takes so much energy to establish 'a truth the size of a pin's head,' then I will leave it to my readers to imagine 'the immense amount of painful research work,' the magnitude of the task I undertook when I started on my quest for truth concerning voice and found that

[1] Published by Cassell & Co., Ltd.

it meant the complete disintegration of the vocal cord legendary mountain. Surely a huge task for one person to undertake. Yet little by little, scrap by scrap, the work has been carried on, and after the abandonment of many false clues, the destruction of many false scents, and the sad burial of many hopes, one can now look back at the forty years of mingled disappointment and success and say that although no claim is made as to finality, yet immense strides towards the ideal of perfection have been made during these years.

To me it has for many years been a matter of absolute wonderment that with all the extraordinary advances made in human knowledge during the last 300 years no one has realized how utterly 'hostile to human progress' is the vocal cord theory of voice. Sir Ronald Ross saved millions of lives by his discovery of the parasite of malaria in the mosquito, and the mode of transmission of that parasite through the insect. When the American, Major Gorgas, went to Panama in order to complete the canal started by de Lesseps he found parks of derelict locomotives and cranes abandoned because of the fearful mortality caused by yellow fever and malaria among the workpeople. Major Gorgas realized that the success of the problem was a medical matter and so began his engineering undertaking by the destruction of the mosquito by petrol, and only advanced with the canal as the tide of disease receded.

> The cunning seeds
> Of million-murdering Death

in this country are not mosquitoes but stale mucus, and through its agency the medical profession gets a very large proportion of its clients. I was, of course, quite prepared to receive and actually have received similar treatment for my mucus theories, to that which was meted to Sir Ronald Ross for his mosquito theories. Inevitably, 'Truth finds foes where it makes none,' and as the French say, *Le vrai n'est pas toujours vraisemblable.*[1] This fact quickly became evident and to many minds I was 'the ramblingest lying rogue on earth.' This, however, did not specially disturb me, for those who knew me better, were quite ready and alert in taking up the cudgels in defence of my work, and carrying the war right into the opposition country.[2] 'Truth,' however, ' is a

[1] Truth does not always seem true.
[2] *Light on the Voice Beautiful, passim.*

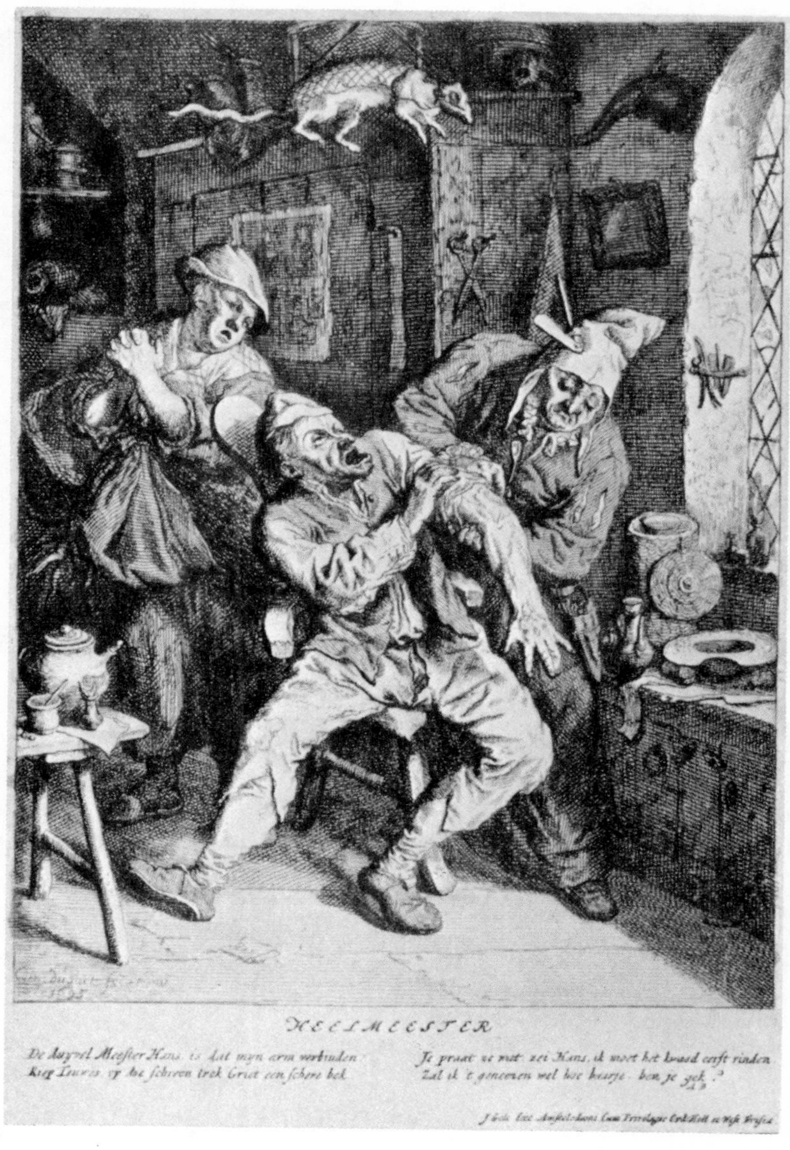

FIGURE 1. SURGEON OPERATING ON A PATIENT'S ARM

From an etching by the Dutch artist, Cornelis Dusart, 1660-1704 daughter of Time,'[1] and when one attempts to overthrow the accepted dogmatism of centuries, it is not reasonable to expect a quick or an easy victory. Treasured traditions hoary with age are not so easily overthrown. 'Thinking,' it has been said, 'is for the few, and claims the few who are out for understanding.'

Has there ever been written a book on the voice by one who really understands the subject? Most authors have based their remarks and teaching on the supposition that tone is produced at the vocal cord centre. No doubt in the minds of many people this supposition amounts to a certainty, but like the late Graham Wallas,

> I believe it is better to insist that the feeling of conviction, like the sensation of sight, is never an infallible guide, and that it only becomes the best guide that we have when it is formed, as Aristotle would say, in the right way and at the right time. We must, that is to say, go behind our feeling of conviction, and ask ourselves whether it was formed under those conditions which experience has shown to be most likely to guard us against error.

The theory of vocal cord sonority owes its origin to the physician Galen (A.D. 130–200). We are fully aware that the correctness of the theory has never been proved, but can we suppose that the orthodox conviction was formed in the second century under 'conditions which are most likely to guard us against error'?

Students know that Galen's writings are simply full of statements which in this twentieth century we know to be erroneous. And no discredit to the worthy physician. Figure 1 gives an idea of a surgical operation as late as the seventeenth century.

Rough and elementary though it appears to our present ideas, yet even then the medical profession had made progress, for in the thirteenth century it was the custom to promote suppuration in treating a wound whether there was foreign matter to be discharged or not, and in the event of a healthy wound not discharging, an irritant was applied to make it do so. Naturally, the medical knowledge of the seventeenth century was no more advanced than the surgical skill. Francis Bacon declares that 'the heart of an ape applied to the neck or head, helpeth the wit, and is good for the falling sickness.' His remedy for warts is more accessible. You simply 'rub the warts with some fat. The fat is then nailed up in the open air, and as the fat wastes away, so the warts diminish.' Such was the elementary and archaic condition

[1] *De waarheid is eene dochter van den tijd.*—Dutch proverb.

of medical matters as late as the seventeenth century. The theory of sound production by the vocal cords dates as we have seen from the third century, and remains perhaps the only topic on which the medical profession is still content with the notions of that time. 'Mankind is a semi-gregarious species,' writes Graham Wallas, 'prone to follow loyalties and solemnities even when the loyalties and solemnities have lost their original usefulness.' The only 'original usefulness' of the vocal cord idea of voice was that 1,700 years ago it lifted the supposed centre for vocalization away from the heart to the throat where it has remained until the present day.

What justification is there for clinging to Galen's theory? Those who do so are not agreed whether the vocal cords act as a stringed instrument, a reed instrument, or on the lines of a siren, that is, a 'puff' instrument. All these theories are taught, notwithstanding the fact that the three kinds of instruments are quite dissimilar in construction and action. The string theory is untenable because (apart from the many other reasons which have had full consideration in my former writings) the vocal cords are at their least tension and thickest when they produce high notes, and at their greatest tension and thinnest when they produce low notes.[1] As regards the reed theory it can hardly be considered a strain on one's intelligence to see that the half-inch of fragile wet tissue which constitutes each vocal cord bears no resemblance of any sort or kind to the brass tongue which is the essential part of an organ reed; further, the reed for a low note must be weighted in order to make it move slowly. The vocal cords have no mechanism which bears the smallest resemblance to such a condition; in fact as already shown, the deeper the note sung the thinner do the cords become, and so act in direct opposition to the theory and practice of an organ reed. With respect to the siren or 'puff' theory, it seems incomprehensible how any thoughtful mind could have found it possible to make any comparison between two pierced metal circular plates which revolve, and two delicate and minute membranes fixed along their whole length and 'frail as the web that misty night has spun.'

Quite apart, however, from the fact that there is not to be found

[1] See *The Brain and the Voice in Speech and Song*, by Dr. F. W. Mott, published by Harper Bros., as well as *Light on the Voice Beautiful*, published by James Clarke & Co., Ltd., p. 83, and Appendix I.

a single point of agreement or similarity between the two, one mechanical detail alone would be fatal to the whole theory. The action of the siren depends entirely upon the revolving plates alternately cutting off the passage of air, and letting it pass when the two holes coincide in their position, one above the other, hence the 'puffs.' As Dr. Holbrook Curtis quite correctly says, the vocal cords 'never touch each other in the middle portion, even in making the initial attack.'[1] hence there must necessarily be a *continuous* flow of air between them, which of course rules out all possibility of comparison with a siren.

These are but a very few of the facts which form the case, on purely scientific grounds, against the hypothesis of vocal cord tone production. In the closing chapter of *Science and Singing* I put the question, 'How can half an inch of wet membranous tissue produce two octaves of sound?' Although the volume has travelled over the world, no one has answered the question.

We have next to enquire whether on practical grounds the vocal cord idea can show any more justification than it does on theoretical grounds, and we begin this enquiry by examining some of the instruction which vocal cord teachers have to offer.

Mr. Ernest Newman, in the *Sunday Times* for 28th March 1926, gives an amusing but absolutely correct account of the difficulties in searching for vocal truth and has most kindly given me permission to copy it.

The article makes an excellent start by referring to a previous critique in which the statement was made 'that what is the matter with ninety-five singers out of a hundred is that they cannot sing.' After which it continues as follows :

> I never cease regretting that Flaubert did not live to finish 'Bouvard et Pécuchet,' and that he did not show us that precious pair working at the science and the art of singing. *Is* it a science or an art would have been the first subject for discussion ; and the authorities on either side would be examined. Then supposing it to be one or the other, or both, or neither, but anyhow something worth trying, what is the secret of the thing? They begin with breathing, they find, each of them, the only correct way according to Smith, or Brown or Jones, as the case may be, but curiously enough, each hopelessly wrong according to Brown, Jones or Smith, or according to Jones, Smith or Brown. Bouvard and Pécuchet try each method in turn, with the only result

[1] *Voice Building and Tone Placing*, by Holbrook Curtis, M.D. Published by J. Curwen & Sons.

of pains in the chest, the ribs or the stomach. Then they get on to the subject of registers. There are two registers, say some of the authors they consult. There are three registers, say others. There is only one register, say others still. Can they all be right, or are they all wrong ? Anyhow Bouvard and Pécuchet try ' producing ' the alleged different sorts of alleged registers, and achieving the alleged ' blending ' of them. Then comes the plaguey problem of breath, ought it to go this way or that, and if so, which, and if not why, and if at all, where ? And the attack. Precisely how should matters be adjusted between the breath stream and the vocal cords ? Should the glottis be shocked, which seems a little cruel, or at the very least immodest, or should more conciliatory methods be tried ? One teacher recommends the glide of the glottis, another the click of the glottis, another the shock of the glottis. All seem to speak with equal authority. Bouvard and Pécuchet click and glide and shock until they get sore throats, but they are as far from singing as ever. And how about the open throat, and nasal resonance (which, of course, must not degenerate into nasal tone), and the Italian vowels, and the position of the head, the shoulders, the ribs, and where the tone ought to come from and where it ought to go, and all the rest of the plaguey problems ? The more they read about them the more confused they get. One authority (I assure the reader I am not romancing) tells the student to ' lean the voice against the back of the eyes ' while another insists that he ought to ' let it flow into the head ' ; another says that the head must be kept up, the arms clear of the ribs, and the weight forward, which hardly seems possible in certain operatic situations, how, for example, is Mme. Jeritza, under these conditions, to sing ' Vissi d'arte ' in the recumbent attitude she does, or Mimi to die in comfort, or Pinkerton and Sharpless to manage the ritual of the whisky-and-soda ? The tongue, again, Bouvard never knew how unruly that member is until he tries to rule it according to the instruction books, and Pécuchet, after trying a few exercises that consist of pushing the tongue out as far as it would go and pulling it back sharply as far as it won't, and lifting it up here and keeping it flat there, finds himself unable to eat any dinner that evening or breakfast next day. They examine their own and each other's throats with the laryngoscope, and come to the conclusion that the less they see of nature's secrets the better for their peace of mind and stomach. Bouvard is sure he has discovered the right method when he comes across the well-known teacher of singing who maintained that the ' sounding-board of the voice is the right leg,' and who ' taught his pupils to stand with the right leg advanced and the weight of the body thrown on it ' ; but Pécuchet practising this in the imaginary role of Mephistopheles walking round the garden with Martha, finds it a little difficult to keep moving gracefully with his right leg always advanced. And the last straw on the back of the harassed pair is when they hear the maid Mélie singing in the kitchen like a canary, though she never read a single treatise on the art (or the science, whichever it is, *if* it is), or had a single lesson on how to ' produce ' her voice.

That Mr. Newman has skilfully and correctly summed up the situation will be clear from the following quotations.

Singing is a great art [says Dr. Irving Voorhees], which does not readily yield to a series of rules and regulations. . . . It is first of all a gift—a gift which is not widely distributed amongst mankind. . . . It is a gift which manifests itself in infancy and *hard work is only a very subordinate qualification* in attaining a great place in the world of song.

This, to begin with, is not very encouraging for the would-be singer, except, indeed, for the lazy and gifted! Pursuing our enquiry we soon come to realize why, apart from Sinus Tone Production, singing is an art which does not yield to rules and regulations. For there is no agreement as to what are the rules. According to Dr. Voorhees,

the voice can be used in two *entirely different* ways—one for the purpose of speech, and the other for expression of the emotions . . . through song.[1]

Dr. Marafioti, in his book on Caruso, gives exactly the opposite opinion:

The two forms of voice, the speaking and the singing, being the same physical element are so closely connected that the neglect of one means the abolition of the proper production and beauty of the other. . . . Scientifically there is no difference between the speaking and the singing voice as physiological phenomena, both being produced by the same vocal organs with an identical mechanism.

Thus, the two medical men, studying the same subject, arrived at exactly opposite conclusions.

The Italian masters [says Dr. Voorhees] spared no pain to 'unite the registers,' dovetailing the one into the other and as it were planing the surface of sound till the voice was smooth and uniform throughout the entire compass and no 'break' or difference of timbre could be detected.

Yet according to Evetts and Worthington,

in so far as it is accepted that the term 'register' refers to a particular laryngeal mechanism, the so-called 'middle' and 'head' registers are not registers at all, but merely different tone qualities due to different positions of the resonator. . . . In singing with the natural voice proper to the sex, differences of register at different points in the compass

[1] *The Hygiene of the Voice*, by Irving Voorhees, M.S., M.D. Published by the Macmillan Co. The italics are mine.

do not occur, and, therefore, no question of the blending of registers should ever arise,[1]

and Dr. Marafioti is clearly in agreement with this theory. But D. A. Clippinger, a practical voice trainer, humorously remarks:

> The statement is frequently made in public print that there are no registers in the trained voice. This order of wisdom is equally scintillating with that profound intellectual effort which avers that a bald headed man has no hair on the top of his head, or that hot weather is due to a rise in the temperature.[2]

Madame Luisa Tetrazzini is in agreement. In her book *How to sing* she writes:

> The question of registers has been the subject of much controversy at various times. There is not even agreement as to how many registers there are or even if there are any at all. . . . Different registers do undoubtedly exist; hence, it is quite a mistake to suggest that the whole notion of registers is a delusion.

It is very interesting that this question of registers is one of the many conflicting vocal doctrines which Sinus principles can elucidate. Those who oppose 'registers' always speak of them as chest, middle and head registers, and they are quite correct in cutting out chest and middle registers, for in fact the whole voice is in the head. Yet the registers most positively exist, but are controlled by making a definite and selective use of the different cavities or sinuses in the head.

Dr. Voorhees is evidently fully aware of the many contradictions which exist in vocal matters, for in his Foreword he says:

> Whence shall come the man who some day is going to be born with a great magic wand which shall unify and intensify and ultimately glorify all of our efforts? Will such a leader ever be able to do away with the chaos now reigning in the fields of Medicine and Music? God grant it speedily.

Dr. Voorhees admits that 'there are some voices which do not develop satisfactorily, where neither the teacher nor the physician can find any discoverable cause for the defect.' Another writer finds that:

> What we do know of the mechanical operations of the voice is exceedingly interesting and a further knowledge of the subject is greatly

[1] *The Mechanics of Singing*, by E. T. Evetts and R. Worthington. Published by J. M. Dent & Sons.

[2] *The Head Voice and Other Problems*. Published by the Oliver Ditson Co.

to be desired. But we can never hope to clear up all the mystery of the vocal action.[1]

These are some of the acknowledged contradictions and limitations of the conventional doctrines of tone production. If we look for plain and definite teaching on what we must do to improve our singing, the results of our search are no more creditable to the vocal cord theory.

Messrs. Chappell & Co. publish a book entitled *Sims Reeves on the Art of Singing*, at the modest price of one shilling. Our English tenor apparently had but little advice to give, for the first edition[2] is contained on twenty-four pages having considerable blank spaces, and one must admit that all his utterances are not exactly great flights of wisdom, even for a shilling! For example:

> Male voices consist of tenors, baritones and basses.

The poor alto was evidently forgotten.

> Falsetto is a false voice as the term implies. . . .
>
> Never take breath in the middle of a word . . . or in the middle of a verb. . . .
>
> The tremolo has no relation to the shake and is only a wobble, very often acquired by making the voice shiver in the jaws. . . .
>
> Pastry is an invention of the enemy—plain food is best.

Rule XVIII states, 'Never sit when practising.' Yet the late Dr. W. H. Cummings, at one time Principal of the Guildhall School of Music, explained to those interested that he always practised sitting sideways on a chair with his right arm hanging over the back of the chair. Evidently one of the 'mysteries of the vocal action.'

Dr. Marafioti gives a rule that 'in taking higher notes of course one must open the mouth a little wider.'[3] Why open the mouth wider, and why 'of course'? On another page he tells us that 'according to the laws of acoustics the larger the size of the instrument the less air is used in producing the sounds.' To this remarkable pronouncement we can only say that the worthy doctor may be an excellent surgeon, but his acoustics are very

[1] *The Psychology of Singing*, by David Taylor. Published by the Macmillan Co.

[2] The only edition published during his life.

[3] *Caruso's Method of Voice Production*. Published by the Appleton Century Co.

much out of repair. Mr. Charles Lunn's advice is perhaps still more mystifying :

> As the larynx ascends in the pipe, the speed of the ascent of the front part of the cricoid is swifter than that of the thyroid ; so that this part of the cricoid in its upward progress gains on the ascent of its auxiliary, the thyroid ; hence the vocal cords are tightened and the pitch of voice raised. In this ascent the thyroid and cricoid rotate on an eccentric centre, causing the planes of both false and true cords to become with each heightened tone more slanting ; thus, the sound, travelling at a right angle to these planes, finds its point of impact on the arch of the palate more and more forward with each ascending sound.[1]

Such involved statements forcibly remind one of what Mr. Ezra Pound terms 'the suffocating morasses of verbiage.' The information may be interesting, but it could hardly be called practical and is more likely to have a bad effect on the tone of a vocalist than a good one. In the art of Sinus Tone Production, no kind of mechanical direction or detail of physiology is given to the student but that which is capable of personal control and application. Mr. Clippinger tells us :

> I was once taught to raise the soft palate until the uvula disappeared. Later I was taught to relax it. Both of these movements of the soft palate were expected to result in a beautiful tone.

The whole larynx is subject to the same contradictory and confusing directions.[2] The mouth, too, comes in for its share of conflicting opinions. Mr. Charles Tree writes, 'Let the mouth take a smiling position ; never forget the smile.'[3] In Mlle. Marchesi's *Vocal Method*[4] the student is told that 'the smiling mouth favoured by many professors past and present is absurd and quite contrary to the laws of acoustics.' But even when tutors are not in direct opposition, the expressions and phrases given for the instruction of the student are utterly nebulous and surrounded by 'a protective vagueness,' to use a Newmanesque expression. 'Sing on the breath ; avoid white voice ; let the tone be round.' The pupil may well ask, 'How can I sing *off* the breath ? If I avoid white voice, am I to produce a voice which is

[1] *The Philosophy of Voice*, by Charles Lunn. Published by Baillière, Tindall & Cox.

[2] See the *Musical Times* for May, June, July and September 1928.

[3] *How to acquire Ease of Voice Production*. Published by Joseph Williams Ltd.

[4] Published by Edwin Ashdown Ltd.

red, black or green? Supposing the tone is not round, will it be square or hexagonal?' Hundreds of examples might be given, and the following is no worse than many others.

> The normal breath-form presents a combination of width and depth that is, a certain amount of lowering of the abdominal wall in the act of inhaling. If, now, the width of the breath-form should be augmented and the depth diminished in proportion, our tone-colour would assume a brighter, perhaps we may call it a more lyrical tone-colour. Now, if we should augment the depth of our breath-form by lowering the abdomen and decrease the width in proportion, our tone-colour would in consequence assume a darker colour.

Surely we may take this as a first-rate example of being, in Shakespearian phrase, 'bethumped with words.' After reading this, the student would of course have full control of 'tone-colour'!

Gladstone was credited with the power of delivering highly involved sentences which expressed very little meaning. On one occasion, so the story states, a bet was made that a question should be put to him, which he would be compelled to answer with a direct reply. The question chosen was, 'Should a clergyman reading the Lessons use the Revised Version?' The following reply was given:

> I am almost inclined to think that a clergyman reading the Revised Version might or might not be considered as almost laying himself open to question as to whether he was or was not putting himself in a doubtful position.

On comparing the two paragraphs it seems to me that the vocal expert should be adjudged the winner, as having said the larger number of words with the less evident meaning. No wonder Matthew Arnold said that the English people lacked the gift of lucidity. No such long procession of words is either permitted or needed to explain Sinus methods. It would be well if authors and speakers would remember that 'words, like glass, darken whatever they do not help us to see.'[1]

A little time since, I was present at a choral rehearsal conducted by a well-known Doctor of Music and cathedral organist. In the midst of the singing, down came the baton with several raps on the desk, and the conductor called out, 'Frying sausages! sing it again!' Another gentleman well-known in musical circles and

[1] Joseph Joubert.

an inspector of music in schools, after hearing a class of girls sing, explained to them, 'Let me have a more beefy tone, I want it more juicy'; whilst a very well-known conductor of my acquaintance told his choir on a certain occasion to 'make a cushion of it.' One might reasonably wonder what the word *it* was intended to represent, but such information was not given. The order consisted simply of five words, neither more nor less. Probably neither of the three gentlemen had read in their Latin classes Quintilian's advice, 'Clearness is the most important thing in the use of words.'[1] A choralist, writing of Sir Hugh Allen, remarks:

> He has a very breezy manner at rehearsals and a wonderful command of similes to illustrate his requirements. It is not always easy to understand his allusions without explanation. A most puzzling remark was once addressed to contraltos—'Sing the next few bars as if you were archbishops!'[2]

In the life of Sir Henry Coward,[3] we are told that at a rehearsal he remarked to the basses, 'You sing it as though you were club-footed.' Now if we realize the importance of 'proper words in proper places' we shall see that neither 'frying sausages,' nor being 'beefy,' 'club-footed' or an 'archbishop,' have any musical significance. Had these gentlemen received an indifferent education, one might have sympathized with them in an endeavour to convey some information to those whom they were training or criticizing. But inasmuch as four out of the five had received a university training, our sympathies go out to the vocalists that their tutors either had such slight acquaintance with the English language or else were so ignorant of the technique of singing that they were unable to find more suitable expressions. Imagine the author of a book being criticized as 'writing as though he were club-footed,' or an artist painting a picture which needed 'more juice,' or a dentist extracting a tooth as though he were an 'archbishop'! All of which goes to show the truth of the statement of Mr. Steuart Wilson, that in singing 'there is no standard technical terminology.'

When we read Dr. Johnson's definition of a network, as 'anything reticulated or decussated at equal distances, with interstices between the intersections,' it may possibly cause a smile, but at

[1] *Perspicuitas in verbis praecipuam habet proprietatem.*
[2] *Daily Telegraph*, 9th August 1930.
[3] By J. A. Rodgers

all events the language is to the point even though involved. But there is no reason why a club-footed man should not be as excellent a vocalist as he has been a poet, nor, so far as we are aware, is there any musical examination for a parson before he can take his seat on the archbishop's throne. In Lord Baldwin's words,' cannot we have done with the spinning of phrases which will not square with the hard facts of life ? '

A free and a pretty imagination is of course frequently helpful in dealing with musical and poetic subjects, but neither ' frying sausages,' nor being ' beefy ' or ' club-footed,' is a pretty figure of speech, nor does the imagery square in the remotest degree with musical matters ; each of the similes only exemplifies ' obscurity illustrated by a further obscurity,' to use a phrase of Edmund Burke, and in the art of training other people, whether children or adults, one cannot afford to be obscure or misleading. Before the end of the first century Tacitus wrote, *Cupidine humani ingenii libentius obscura creduntur.*[1] In the twentieth century all the arts and sciences have escaped from the bondage of muddle and confusion except voice, which remains in ' the era of anyhow,' to use another expression of Lord Baldwin.

A well-known writer once declared, ' There are but three classes of men, the retrograde, the stationary, and the progressive.' Teachers of singing may be divided likewise into three classes. The first consists of those who teach in a sort of happy-go-lucky way, without any attempt at method or science. The pupil merely sings a scale or two either in tune or not, and then proceeds to as many songs as can be conveniently sung in the twenty or thirty minutes, *lesson.* Such was one of my tutors at the musical establishment that honoured me by taking my fees. We cannot criticize these ladies and gentlemen in detail because they have no detail ; they make no pretence of being ' a voice-producer.' In Sir Henry Wood's *The Gentle Art of Singing* ' the " Voice-producer " with his attendant terrors is discomfited and banned in no uncertain terms.'[2] Well, these people in our Class I will certainly not come within the scope of Sir Henry's ban. So long as the would-be singer ' produces ' the necessary cheque for the

[1] ' Through the eagerness of the human mind, things obscure are too readily believed.' See *Light on the Voice Beautiful*, page 152 *a*. Page 152 *a* refers to the upper part of page 152. The letter *b* would refer to the lower half of the page.

[2] So writes a reviewer in the *Dominant*.

so-called lessons, that is the one outstanding part of the bargain between pupil and teacher. These 'professors' usually are thoroughly good-natured people and excellent company; they have chosen 'music' as a means of livelihood, they usually have a voice like a bull of Bashan and use it accordingly, and that's that. But 'surely one of the most delectable bees that ever buzzed in any bonnet is the old dream that in art the right thing to do is to do without workmanship. . . . To sing—all with your soul alone without the tainted assistance of any mere technical methods.'[1]

The second group is worthy of more respect, for its members frequently have devoured many books in order to learn some of the long names which the medical practitioner has given to those parts of our anatomy which are more or less connected with voice. Then from this same medical and anatomical point of view it must be, of course, a matter of importance for the student to know how the diaphragm, the floating ribs and the thyroid cartilage act; further, he must try to determine what decision to make about the much discussed *coup de glotte*. Should the glottis be 'shocked' or not? Garcia prescribes the method 'as the best means of purifying and strengthening the vocal tones,' whilst Dr. Holbrook Curtis says that 'the "coup de glotte" is death to the voice; it is born of ignorance and to teach or allow its continuance is a crime.' Then the tongue. How much ink has been used in writing about it since Saint James declared it to be an 'unruly member'! Well, Madame Lilli Lehmann says, 'the tongue must generally form a furrow . . . without the furrow, no tone—except the very highest—is perfect in its resonance, none can make full use of it.' Mr. Clippinger pointedly declares that grooving the tongue 'is no more scientific than kicking the cat out of your way if she gets under your feet.'

Thus once more we are faced with the irreconcilable contradictions which baffle every attempt to understand the vocal cord 'method' of singing. If the conscientious tutors of our second group unfortunately make the wrong choice amongst these alternatives, what are their pupils to do? We need not wonder if they adopt in despair the attitude of a correspondent in the *Musical Times* who wrote: 'As I view the matter, good voice

[1] *A Writer's Notes on his Trade*, by C. E. Montague. Published by Chatto & Windus.

production is a *knack* to be acquired by the most primitive of methods—trial and error—extended over a considerable time. . . . The cure for bad teaching must be with the pupil. Let him do as Santley did—pay off and dismiss an unsatisfactory teacher.'[1] But what an alarming prospect for the would-be vocalist. Clearly time and money under such conditions must be accounted of no value in the attempt to learn to sing. What would become of our eyesight if we had no better means of getting some glasses to enable us to see our music? We should quickly lose what sight we have, and vocal wreckage is only too frequently the lot of the singing student. Nor is this a matter for surprise when we consider the conflicting theories. Here indeed

> Chaos umpire sits,
> And by decision more embroils the fray
> By which he reigns; next him high arbiter
> Chance governs all.

At a recent conference of the Incorporated Society of Musicians, one gentleman present expressed the opinion that 'there is no right way or wrong way of singing.' He did not give any explanation of this remark, and it would not be worth chronicling but for the fact that the statement was made at a representative body of voice specialists. Equally helpless was another gentleman who asked the assembled company if anyone present could give him the 'three correct rules for the Old Italian method of singing.' He explained that he had studied in Italy and remembered two rules which were (1) *The louder the note the fuller the tone*; and (2) *The higher the note the fuller the tone.* From these interesting and elegant rules, it would appear that the gentleman had not lost much by forgetting the third. At all events no one seemed able to help him.[2]

Certain minds having observed 'the awful conflict' and possibly the hopeless stupidities in the theories of vocal training, together with the practical results on voices 'riven with vain endeavour,' conceived the idea of training by imitation. These tutors make a third class. Jean de Reszke adopted this line of action in his Paris school. He would say, 'I can imitate you, why can you not imitate me?' Had he asked me that question I should have replied that it was a much easier matter for a good voice to

[1] W. R. Leaver, March 1932.
[2] See Appendix II.

imitate a bad or a poor one, than for a poor voice to imitate a good one. In some respects this class of tutor is more logical and to be better trusted than either of the others. Having observed the hopelessness of suggesting any analogy between the human voice, and organ, violin or siren, they therefore advise the student to *think* of beautiful tone, to imagine beautiful tone, in the hope that the mentality will produce beautiful tone. This attitude has one very great advantage inasmuch as it can never do harm, or produce a strain. Indeed, we willingly go further and admit that in some cases actual good has resulted, because the quiet and restful quality of voice which the student has produced, has developed a certain amount of strength and possibly even control, which was not present before the lessons. The objections to the system, if ' system ' it can be called, are, however, many. It premises that the student is able to produce a beautiful tone, and the premise is frequently at fault and without any foundation. The poor student is only too willing and eager to produce a really beautiful sound. His mind is absolutely full of it, but he has no notion what to do or how to act in order to change his hard and unmusical voice into a thing of charm and beauty. Needless to say his tutor is equally ignorant, and in many cases blames the pupil for having an unmusical ear, whereas the pupil is every bit as conscious of the failure as the teacher.

The idea of the tutors in this class finds expression in Clippinger's book, *The Head Voice and Other Problems*. ' The most beautiful tone,' he writes, ' is the most perfectly produced, whether the singer knows anything of vocal mechanism or not. In such a tone there is no consciousness of mechanics or scientific laws. The vocal mechanism is responding automatically to the highest law in the universe—the law of beauty.' These statements are in the main true, but let us closely examine them. Obviously ' the most beautiful tone is the most perfectly produced.' ' Beauty is truth, truth beauty,' wrote Keats, but neither the poet nor the instructor gives the necessary rules which the student must observe and carry out in order to ensure the production of tone which is beautiful because ' perfectly produced.' Mr. Clippinger stresses the necessity of thinking of good tone and of ' relaxation,' but important as these details are, they are insufficient in themselves to ensure the production of ' beautiful tone.'

Up to the present the few people who have been able to produce 'the most beautiful tone' certainly have had no knowledge of scientific laws. Sims Reeves, Plunket Greene, Adelina Patti, Albani, Tetrazzini, Caruso, amongst vocalists, and the late Dr. McNaught, Albert Visetti, Sir Edward Bairstow, Sir Henry Wood, David Taylor, and D. A. Clippinger, amongst vocal tutors, have each denied all knowledge of scientific singing for voice culture. Even the 'Swedish Nightingale,' who was both a world-renowned vocalist and a tutor, seemed to be no better informed, for according to Liza Lehmann, Jenny Lind informed her that she sang with the uvula! Obviously it is possible to sing without any definite knowledge of acoustic laws, but how many thousands of students having no surer guide than a concept of the desired result have failed to produce beautiful tone in consequence of their ignorance of the very laws by which beautiful tone is produced? What architect could design and control the building of a magnificent cathedral, without knowledge of scientific laws acquired through long and most careful training? What sort of a picture would the person produce who used paint and brush without any technical knowledge and study? Yet we are continually told that in order to produce a beautiful note the main point is to *think* it. 'A tone exists first as a mental concept and the quality of the mental concept determines the quality of the tone. . . . No one will ever sing a better tone than the one he thinks.'[1]

Undoubtedly the last statement is correct, but it is only a small part of the truth, for it is equally certain that one may make a mental picture of a tone which is vastly better than that which he is able to produce, so we see the mental concept does not necessarily determine the quality of the tone. If it did, we must come to the conclusion that Sir Henry Wood, Dr. A. H. Mann and Viola Tree—to mention only three—were incapable of thinking of beautiful tone! The idea is too preposterous. Sir Henry Wood admits the poor quality of his voice; and on an occasion when the late Dr. Mann was speaking before the Incorporated Society of Musicians, he told his audience that if ever at King's College, he attempted at choir practice to sing a phrase to his choir boys, they would at once begin to titter! If thinking a beautiful note would produce it, then undoubtedly the organist

[1] D. A. Clippinger, *op. cit.*

of King's College, Cambridge, and our famous orchestral conductor, would have been two of the most prominent vocalists in Europe.

It may well be said that a tone 'exists first as a mental concept,' but one may have the mental concept of a really fine voice, and yet be as ignorant of how to produce it 'as a Hottentot is of Calvinism.'[1] It is true that we are not likely to sing a beautiful tone if we think of an ugly one, but there are thousands of people who will think of a beautiful tone but at the same time sing an exceedingly ugly one, because they do not in the least know how to act or what course to pursue in order to produce a sound which even approaches the beautiful. I shall never forget the exquisite violin tone produced by Kreisler the first time I heard him play, but the 'mental concept' of that tone would never enable me to play the violin. To become a violinist one *must* acquire a thorough technique of the instrument through years of patient practice. The sole reason that Sir Percy Buck, for example, has never been able to sing is the utter lack of technical vocal instruction he was able to get.[2]

One other matter remains to be dealt with before we leave our consideration of the imitative or 'mental concept' school of singing. In the book from which I have already quoted, Clippinger writes:

> If a listener knows when his voice sounds right he knows it entirely separate and apart from any knowledge he may have of its scientific construction; hence such knowledge is of no value whatever in determining what is good and what is bad in tone quality. A tone is not a thing to see, and the teacher cannot use a camera and a manometric flame in teaching tone production. . . . Vocal organs are no more alike than are eyes, noses and hands.

With respect to the manometric flame, I can quite believe that the vocal student who works on larynx theories would find no assistance from manometric flames, but every pupil who understands Sinus principles will benefit very considerably by studying the acoustic principles which govern the changes that take place in manometric flames.[3] Up to the present the camera has not been of any use in vocal matters, but that is only because the photographer has been unable to show me what I want. If some scientist

[1] To borrow D. A. Clippinger's simile.

[2] See *Light on the Voice Beautiful*, page 27, and Appendix III.

[3] See *Science and Singing*, page 30, and Appendix IV.

will build me a camera which will show me the exact number and relative sizes of the sinuses, and if possible their condition, I think I can safely guarantee a very valuable and useful addition to camera work.

Finally, we easily agree that the 'vocal organs are no more alike than are eyes, noses and hands.' This undoubtedly is correct. But another side of the truth and a supremely important one, is that the vocal organs are no *less* alike than are eyes, noses and hands. I have enquired of Messrs. Steward & Son, opticians in the Strand, London, and they tell me that in all their considerable experience they have never found the two eyes of one person identical with the two eyes of any other, but the laws of optics applied to sight are so definite and the mechanics are of such precision that the various defects of vision can be corrected with the most minute exactitude, and with a modern retinoscope it is easy now to test the eyes of a foreigner or a deaf person. Obviously a similar line of thought is applicable to the whole human body; otherwise anatomy could be neither taught nor learned, and operations for appendicitis and other troubles would be quite impossible. We therefore are bound to conclude that although the 'vocal organs are no more alike than are eyes and noses,' that does not exclude a scientific method in dealing with them. We will proceed to the next point.

We have found so far that there is no valid ground, either in theory or in practice for continuing to give credence to Galen's theory of voice production. We have seen that there is no tuition to be had from his disciples to which we could submit with any sort of confidence. Such a conclusion brings us face to face with a question which will probably be already springing to the reader's mind: 'What of the great singers of the past? Do they not demonstrate the accuracy of the accepted theories of voice?' This question has been so often propounded as a criticism of the Sinus Tone Production theory, that I am going to try to bring together here enough facts to answer it once and for all. What light, then, does the history of vocalism really throw upon the matter?

In the early sixties Jenny Lind told Eduard Hanslick that the art of singing had gone to the dogs, that there were then only shriekers and howlers. That was at the dawn of Patti's fame. The truth of the matter is that for centuries each generation has had its few good singers and its many bad. Richard Wagner suffered considerably through unsatisfactory vocalists. At the first performance of *Tannhäuser* at the Court Theatre in Munich in 1855, the performance was marred by an incompetent tenor in the leading part. Worse trouble was experienced three years later when *Lohengrin* appeared, for we read that only two of the soloists 'were even moderately capable of doing justice to their parts.'[1] *The Flying Dutchman*, which was first produced in 1843, had its performance in Munich in 1864, and 'the singers were fairly satisfactory.' In September 1878, at Berlin, *Siegfried* had its first performance with the name part taken by Jäger, who was 'hoarse and sang consistently out of tune.' We should doubtless have been in ignorance about these wretched vocalists but for the important fact that Wagner's operas were being brought before the public for the first time and therefore a full account of the performances was necessary. Looking further back still, we find that until the end of the sixteenth century the art of solo singing had hardly any existence. Up to that date composers wrote polyphonic works which demanded a chorus for their presentation. solo singing had no home or school for its development, but was carried on as a tradition by the troubadours and wandering minstrels. It was Claudio Monteverdi's production of the operas *Arianna* and *Orfeo*, on similar lines to Peri's *Euridice* produced seven years earlier, which created a demand for solo singers, and by the middle of the seventeenth century there must have been some very fine solo singers if we may judge by the elaborate music written for them.

This is just a reasonable supposition, but it is a historical fact that the great Faustina Bordoni in 1716 was creating wonderment and astonishment in Italy by her marvellous singing. Contemporary with her was the celebrated *basso* Giuseppe Boschi, who was probably the original Polifeme of Handel's *Aci, Galatea e Polifeme*. It is said that he was the only bass at that time who was capable of singing that music. It is thus evident that good voices were not numerous in the eighteenth century any more than they are in the twentieth century. A further detail worthy of consideration is the fact that this gentleman, a tailor in his early life, was not likely to have spent very much time and money for the

[1] *Fact and Fiction about Wagner*, by Ernest Newman. Published by Cassell & Co., Ltd.

purpose of developing a voice, but was almost certainly in the same category as Jenny Lind, Tetrazzini, and many others, namely, a heaven-born vocalist. In the same list must be placed Lucrezia Agujari, who in 1764 at the age of twenty-one made a triumphant début in Florence. On the authority of no less a critic than Mozart, she could sing well from middle C to A *in altissimo*.

Two years after the birth of Agujari, Germany produced the famous bass, Ludwig Fischer, with a compass of Closely following on was Brigitta Banti, another vocal genius, who began life as a street singer, but at the age of nineteen was singing in opera at Paris. This brings us to 1778, and Banti's extraordinary career finishes in the nineteenth century, when that of Malibran, daughter of Manuel Garcia, began. She made her début at the age of seventeen in June 1825. Luigi Lablache, the celebrated *basso*, fourteen years her senior, began his professional career at the age of eighteen in opera at Naples.

It is not of course our object here to give an account of the lives of the great singers of the past, but it is instructive to consider some of the important details which history has given to us. Of these facts there are two which are specially interesting in the life of Lablache. The first is that at the San Carlino Theatre where he was singing, his voice was the only one out of the whole company that withstood the ordeal of giving two performances daily. Thus we see that voices were ruined long before the twentieth century. The second point is that he published a *Méthode de Chant*, but we learn from *Grove's Dictionary of Music* that 'it rather disappointed expectation.' No doubt it did.

The seventeenth and eighteenth centuries had their few outstanding vocalists who were each and all simply heaven-born singers, and had no definite 'method' to hand down to posterity. Amongst these singers of earlier days it is of course chiefly their successes which achieve remembrance. But when it comes to our own day, we can recall that Herr Tauber, Mr. Paul Robeson, and Madame Lotti Lehmann, each had recently a breakdown. In June 1932, Mr. Arthur Fear had a second time to retire from his engagement in the title-role of *Casanova* at the Coliseum. In 1933, Frida Leider was suddenly unable to sing as Isolde at Covent Garden Opera House, her place being taken by the Cologne soprano Henny Trundt who flew to London to deputize for her, arriving only in time to go straight to the performance. On 8th May 1935, Torsten Ralf, a Swedish tenor, flew from Frankfurt to Croydon in order to take the place of the Swiss tenor, Max Hirzel, who had rehearsed the part of Lohengrin, 'but was prevented by a cold' from fulfilling his engagement. In May 1936 the singing of Mr. Bockelmann who was cast for the part of Wotan at Covent Garden was through his indisposition 'a semi-fiasco' according to a correspondent of the *Daily Telegraph*. The list of failures could be lengthened. We have some earlier examples. Blanche Marchesi, in *Singer's Pilgrimage*,[1] relates how in America she lost the opportunity of an engagement at the Metropolitan Opera House, because when Mr. Gatti Casazza came to see her, she had been eating ices, and so, 'I had not a sound in my throat,' she writes. 'Such disappointments,' she continues, 'will occur often in an artist's life, but I must say mine was *strewn with them*.'

The late Sir Charles Santley, in his *Reminiscences*,[2] gives another example: 'Isabella Alba, a very charming singer and intelligent actress, I thought was destined to rise to a high position, but an affection of the throat compelled her to abandon the stage after a short career.' She afterwards 'devoted herself to teaching.' Nor is the musical profession the only one that suffers in this manner. In political circles it is well known that Viscount Snowden held the parliamentary record for inaudibility. Mr. Lloyd George's voice gave out altogether in one of his Budget speeches, and Mr. Balfour moved the adjournment for a couple of hours to allow him to recover. Teachers, clergy, and others whose work depends upon their speech are similarly liable to meet with disaster.

It becomes evident then, that if the vocal cord theory is to be given credit for the 'great singers of the past' it must take the responsibility also for many who were not successful. 'Voices fail by the hundreds because of false methods, and singers whose natural gifts would entitle them to a long and glorious career, are compelled to abandon singing after a few years of painful struggle and devote themselves, in most cases, to the profession of teaching.'[3] But some of the examples given already raise doubts

[1] Published by Grant Richards.
[2] Published by Edward Arnold.
[3] Dr. Marafioti.

whether the vocal cord idea can even claim the credit for past successes.

Gifted singers have invariably been more interested in interpretation and the choice of songs than in the theory of singing or the elucidation of its technical problems. According to Plunket Greene, ' where the voice is *produced* goodness knows ; the singer certainly does not.' Patti when asked about her singing would reply, ' I know nothing about it,' and Emmy Destinn was no clearer in her ideas. Patti, in the opinion of both William Kuhe and Julius Benedict, would have been the greatest singer of the nineteenth century even if she had never received a single lesson in vocalization. As she herself declared that she never practised technical exercises for more than ten minutes a day, the opinion is no doubt correct. The world-renowned Madame Galli-Curci never received any instruction in the art of singing. Nevertheless she could draw and thrill an audience of 2,000 people. Sir Charles Santley expressed himself in terms similar to those of Plunket Greene : 'How the voice is produced or where, except that it is through the passage of the throat, is unimportant.' Obviously neither Signor Nava nor any other tutor could have given him much instruction in vocal technique during his long stay in Italy. When in Milan, he went, following the advice of Sims Reeves, to Lamperti for lessons.

> We were shown into a room [he writes] where the professor was giving a lesson to a somewhat vulgar-looking woman, who emitted the most agonizing shrieks, I thought. I also thought if that were Mr. Lamperti's method of teaching, I would not trouble him for his instruction.

Fortunate it was for Charles Santley that even in his early days, he was critical of the tuition he received. Yet being critical could not make up for the lack of good instruction, and even Santley suffered from that, as the following experience shows :

> At the general rehearsal[1] I was so nervous I sang *Il balen* nearly half a note sharp throughout. I was perfectly aware of it myself, but could not come down.

No Sinus student would ever be placed in such a predicament.

We can hardly conclude this consideration of the ' great singers of the past ' without referring to the most widely renowned of them all.

[1] At Covent Garden

> Caruso [writes Dr. Marafioti] had nothing exceptional in his laryngeal apparatus, and the larger size of his vocal cords or other peculiarities which have been mentioned about his vocal organs were certainly not the decisive elements in his phenomenal singing. On the contrary, there were shortcomings in his throat which were so evident that if he had had to rely on his vocal organs alone for his career he would perhaps never have become a singer at all. . . . His throat was not the magic organ that gave rise to his greatness.

Was he, then, exceptionally well trained ? One detail in his Italian 'training' consisted of placing the crown of his head against a wall and then starting his practice. There is no difficulty in accepting Marafioti's opinion, that

> if at the beginning of his career Caruso failed to do justice to his vocal gift, he was unconsciously the *victim* of technical influences imposed on him by his teachers.

But apparently he did not remain long a victim, for Pierre Key tells us that when he was asked, 'What did you do to make so secure and formidable your high notes ?' he replied, 'Do you want the truth ? Well, I will give it you. Instead of following all the suggestions of my teachers, I did just the opposite.' It is possible that in accepting this story we should make some allowance for conceit, but after all it corresponds to Jean de Reszke's claim that he obtained 'very little help from his teachers.' And Caruso expressed the same belief more seriously when he remarked:

> One may see that there are actually as many methods as there are singers, and any particular method, even if accurately set forth, might be useless to the person who tried it. . . . My own particular way of singing, *if I have any*, is after all, particularly suited to me only.

Marafioti's own conclusion is that

> the belief that the vocal cords of singers are responsible for the power and the beauty of their voices, and are the source of their exceptional singing, is as false as it is popular. . . . It is universally known that most of the greatest singers never knew how they produced their voices. . . . Caruso himself tried to investigate his own voice, but his analysis was fruitless. His marvellous singing was natural, eminently natural, and his voice production *could not be governed by any* conscious influence.

His want of success in this particular endeavour was well emphasized by his complete failure in the one and only attempt he ever made as a tutor. Pierre Key in his life of Caruso[1] tells us that the

[1] Published by Hurst & Blackett.

great tenor would sit for over an hour at a piano 'thumping clumsily a few simple chords,' whilst the pupil, a man with a fine baritone voice, endeavoured to imitate his master's voice, but without the smallest success. There is excellent ground for stating that many voices have suffered in the endeavour to imitate Caruso, whilst his success was due largely to his own personal perception and initiative. It is therefore abundantly clear that no definite scientific system or carefully laid plan could be credited with the wonderful vocal development of any of these great artists.[1] Aristotle said that without generalization there is no science, and when we understand that 'the greatest singers never knew how they produced their voices,' it becomes quite evident that the heaven-born vocalist has nothing to teach us in the matter of a definite or scientific voice control, and his lack of precise method is neither an inconvenience nor an annoyance to him, until an attack of laryngitis, nodes on the vocal cords, inflamed tonsils or some other disturbance in that particular region, interferes with the correct and what hitherto has been the normal working of the vocal machine.

By whatever test we apply, the idea of vocal cord tone production is shown to be untenable,[2] while the theory of Sinus Tone Production answers every question and solves every difficulty. Vocal cord sonority is nothing but an antique tradition ; Sinus Tone Production is a hypothesis formulated in this century as a result of exhaustive investigations and practical experience. By the exponents of vocal cord methods, the voice is not looked upon as a scientific subject. This opinion is held by American, Italian, French and English writers. It is possible that authors of other nationalities may also agree, but I know of Dr. Voorhees and David Taylor in America, of Sir Edward Bairstow, Howard Fry and Field-Hyde in England, of Dr. Guillemin in France. Considering that theirs is a system which 'might be useless to the person who tried it,' their conclusion is inevitable. But Sinus theories claim to be scientific and provide a method of training which is trustworthy, understandable, and of universal validity. The conventional methods have ruined countless voices, and have only a very dubious claim to the credit for great successes ; by

[1] The list of illustrations is by no means exhausted by those given here. Further examples are to be found in my previous writings.

[2] See Appendix V.

contrast a training in Sinus Tone Production is effecting an improvement in every voice to which it is applied, restoring those which have failed through other methods, and literally creating singers out of average, unselected, but keen students.

Young singers who are gifted with voices of exceptional promise quite naturally go for their training to one of the schools of music where vocal scholarships are to be gained, and whose influence may help them in starting on their careers. But the training received should be judged by the general level of vocal attainment shown by the students rather than by the brilliance of one or two outstanding scholars. A few years ago, with these considerations in mind, I published an offer (and, I may say, it is still open), which I was impelled to make by a lecture delivered to the singing students of the Royal Academy by Mr. Howard Fry.[1]

At the outset he admitted that ' the art of voice production is not at present an exact science.' He continued :

> It is true that, while we have many successes amongst students here (and the same may be said of most other similar institutions throughout the empire), in all honesty we have to record many failures.

This he afterwards admitted to be ' a sad state of affairs,' and he proceeded to give his reasons for the ' sad ' condition. From my personal point of view the reasons suggested were illogical and unsatisfactory. I therefore ventured to suggest to Mr. Fry and to the Principal of the Royal Academy of Music, that I should take three out of the ' many failures ' and give them free tuition for a year. At the end of that time, independent experts should test their vocal powers and report whether they must still be placed in the same category as failures. My letter finished as follows :

> I am the only person who can lose by the proposition. If my work in training be judged a failure, I not only lose twelve months' work with the three students, but much more, I lose prestige and credit with my numerous followers who believe in Sinus Tone Production. The Royal Academy comes out on top either way. If I fail it will have the credit of proving that so far nothing better has been evolved than the precepts of the old Italian masters, notwithstanding their acknowledged incompleteness. If I succeed, then the Royal Academy will have the credit for being the first college in the world fearlessly to stand forth and with an open mind test the system which deserves testing ; and as a Royal school will have the satisfaction of leading where eventually others will be compelled to follow.

[1] See the *Lecture Recorder*, July 1932.

My suggestion was not accepted, the Principal declining even to discuss any matter with me.

One might have thought that knowing the existence of ' many ' vocal failures, the Academy pedagogues might have been glad to offer another opportunity to some of the many who, having paid for their tuition, yet failed to get the hoped for result. The *quid pro quo* was conspicuous by its absence. This certainly is not the case with those who study Sinus methods. If this particular school is at present unable to point to international artists as the result of its training, yet it has students who have with great success taken the solo parts in Bach's B minor *Mass*, *The Messiah*, *The Creation*, *Elijah* and other works of sacred music, as well as in Coleridge-Taylor's *Tale of Old Japan*, and many operas and other secular works ; besides taking the ' duds ' from several of the well-known schools, and turning them into satisfactory vocalists with melodious and well-balanced voices. These people studied singing simply from the love of it, and had no wish to become professionals, and therefore do not come into the eye of the public. ' The right to rebellion is the right to seek a higher rule and not to wander in mere lawlessness,' wrote George Eliot. I venture to make the claim, and the claim has been substantiated,[1] that Sinus Tone principles, although a ' rebellion ' against vocal cord ideas, are founded upon and are in accordance with scientific and acoustic laws and therefore are a ' higher ' rule, and the more closely the theory is examined and the more it is tested, the more inescapable do its conclusions become.

[1] See *Light on the Voice Beautiful*, *passim*.

CHAPTER II

THE TECHNIQUE OF SINUS TONE PRODUCTION

Thought is the property of those only who can entertain it.—Emerson.

Dr. Voorhees commences his valuable book, *The Hygiene of the Voice*, as follows: 'The first question that every candidate for vocal honours should ask himself or herself, is, "Is my voice worthy of cultivation?"'

I am frequently asked the question, 'Is my voice worth training?' My reply is always the same: 'That is a matter for you to determine.' Every voice is worthy of cultivation, every voice is worth improving and ought to be made beautiful and pleasing, but it is not every one who cares to spend time and money on the improvement. Such an annoyance as a harsh unmusical voice should not and need not exist throughout the world. The worse the condition of the voice, the more it needs training, both for aesthetic and health reasons; for a harsh voice is just as certain an indication that readjustments are wanted in the vocal mechanism as squeaking machinery is that examination and assistance from the engineer are required. If the mechanic understands the machine to which he is called, he gets rid of the friction and the machine runs smoothly with its maximum efficiency. In the same way the Sinus tutor with a few simple rules carefully expressed and intelligently applied can enable every voice to be developed to its utmost beauty and power.

In the twenty-nine years which have passed since the first edition of *Science and Singing* appeared, I have been able by careful thought and persistent observation to formulate a number of principles which, if understood and acted upon, will carry the student towards that glorious land of song where only the beautiful is heard, and where jars, blemishes and breakdowns are practically unknown. 'Simplicity is the foundation of all art,' said Plunket Greene, and the road laid out for the Sinus Tone Production traveller is free from all traps and snares; but it is only right to add that much patience and much perseverance will be required.

The rules which are so easy to understand will not work automatically and become a natural part of the singer's equipment unless considerable time is spent on the endeavour. Some people advance more quickly than others, and so reach their destination while others are still plodding on, but the great joy is to know that none, however slow, need despair of a successful journey or doubt the happiness of its ultimate conclusion.

The work of the vocal tutor is far more than the mere criticism of result. In many cases, possibly in the majority, the pupil knows when a note is harsh or out of tune just as well as the master ; but the student is unaware of the cause, and this is where the teacher of Sinus theories shows his power of tuition. It is indeed one of the first duties of the Sinus tutor to impress on his pupil the fact that he has not come to the lesson for the purpose of learning to *sing*, but to learn the *control of the machine* which creates singing. If the student produces an unsatisfactory note, then the law of causality is invoked ; and it is the duty of the master to explain in simple non-technical terms exactly *why* the note is incorrect, and by what means it may be improved and eventually made as nearly perfect as the given vocal machine is capable of making it. Thus while the vocal student on orthodox lines is faced with a bewildering mass of contradictions, Sinus theories teach the student how to develop the voice to the very fullest extent by acoustic and controllable laws, which are at his service when he understands them. The rule which I have previously expressed is always observed : ' First the scientific mechanic, then the glorious artist, beautiful and free.' Under these conditions the future of vocalism is brighter than it has ever been before, because the laws which govern the voice have now been formulated and tested.

The voice-producing instrument[1] consists of a series of cranial cells, or ' sinuses,' situated as shown in Figure 2 on page 30. These are arranged in two sets in the left and right sides of the skull, just as we have two eyes and twin nostrils. The frontal sinuses lie just above the eyebrow ridge. Immediately behind the frontal sinuses and in direct communication with them, are groups of cells known as the anterior ethmoid cells. Behind these

[1] For a full description of the vocal machine, the reader must turn to *Science and Singing*, which is illustrated by many photographs. Only a brief résumé of that description can be given here, before we pass to more detailed considerations.

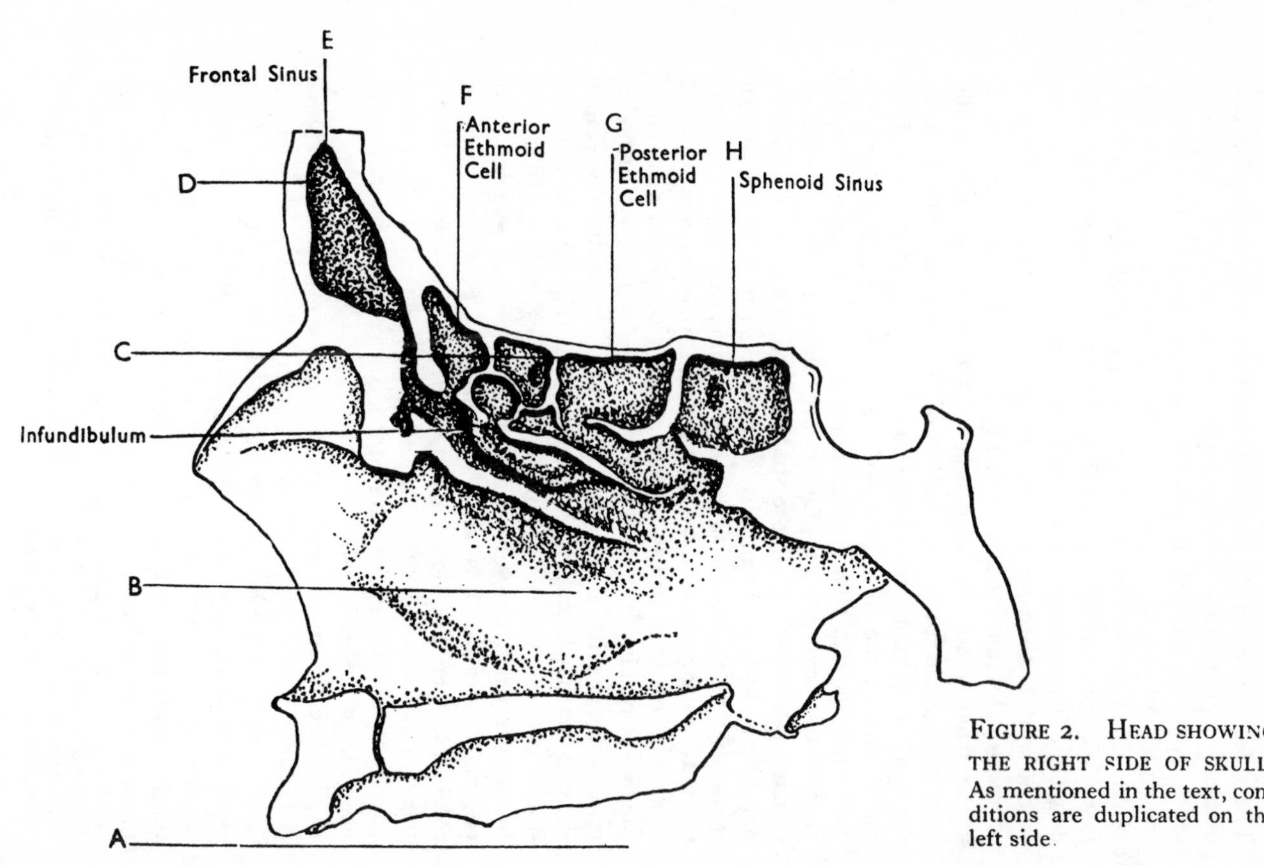

FIGURE 2. HEAD SHOWING THE RIGHT SIDE OF SKULL. As mentioned in the text, conditions are duplicated on the left side.

again, come the middle and the posterior ethmoid cells, each having a separate opening into the nasal cavity. Lastly there are the sphenoid sinuses to the rear of the ethmoid cells. This, very briefly, is a description of the fully developed adult sinus system In different heads there is scope for material variation in the number, size and shape of the various cells, in their exact relative positions and in the openings which connect them with the nasal cavity. Hence arises the infinite variety of voices of which we are all aware. In the fully developed voice all the different sinuses are brought into use all the time ; but the focus of activity changes according to the pitch of the voice, the highest notes requiring the biggest proportion of frontal sinus activity. Very few voices, however, are fully developed. In the vast majority of cases among ordinary people only a part of the vocal instrument is used[1] either in speaking or singing, the part which most readily falls into disuse, simply because of its remoteness and its tortuous entries, being the frontal sinus pair. Consequently, the technique of the Voice Beautiful may be defined in one phrase as the process of bringing under separate control and afterwards blending together the activity of the air in all the four sets of sinuses.

The purpose of this chapter is to explain that process. To this end, the first point is to show that the air in the head can be brought under control. The whole fabric of Sinus Tone Production depends on this initial step, and it is a step which is not understood or thought of either by the vocal cord teacher of singing, or by the medical man or the professor of acoustics. I therefore propose to take the matter step by step (although it is possible that to some readers the steps may appear unnecessarily small), as I want this volume to be helpful to the beginner, as well as to the experienced student.

I would therefore ask the reader to get a vase, and holding it upside down, blow with lips well pointed forward across its base. The result of this will be that the breath striking the vase disperses and is soon at rest. Now reverse the vase, and direct the breath with pointed lips so as to form a moving column of air which strikes the inner edge of the vase. In this case the column of air is not dispersed, but moving and vibrating in an enclosed space produces a musical sound. Now let the reader transfer his

[1] With results which may be serious, quite apart from the question of vocalism : see Chapter III.

attention from the vase to himself. First direct a column of air out of the mouth. This of course is easily accomplished and silence is the result, because the breath is moving through a space which is not enclosed. Now direct the breath downwards from the nose, and we have the same result through the same cause, namely, the air moving in an unenclosed space. Now move a trifle higher and create an air movement just above the nose, that is to say in the sinuses, and you must have sound because the breath, that is the air, is moving in a small confined space. Thus we have voice. We have, then, four air levels in the head, viz.: the lowest in the mouth below the hard palate; the second level in the nose above the hard palate; and the two upper in the sinuses above the nasal position. It is obvious that we can at will actuate the air in the low and second levels, and bearing in mind that air moving in a confined space must produce sound, it becomes apparent that we can at will actuate the air in the two higher levels, and thus at will produce voice.[1]

In dealing with pupils I always use the idea of an air movement being initiated by means of an electric current coming from the brain where the vagus and spinal accessory nerves have their origin,[2] and I believe that eventually a full and convincing explanation will be found of all those details which at the moment are considered by the electrical expert to be a stumbling-block to the full acceptance of Sinus theories of voice. Of this I am fully convinced, but the method of approach which I have just described does away with the *necessity* of the electric theory, but emphasizes in its place the acknowledged idea that our functions and activities are directed by the mind or will. Every one knows full well the effect that the body has on the mind, but there are very many who do not yet realize the controlling effect which the mind has on

[1] I am aware that this exposition does not constitute a proof of the theory of Sinus Tone Production. But experiment will carry conviction.

[2] My idea, first mentioned in the 1918 edition of *The Voice Beautiful*, that the functioning of the brain is accompanied and characterized by electric currents has been endorsed by Dr. A. E. Kornmueller of the Kaiser Wilhelm Institute for Brain Research in Berlin. In a special cable to the *New York Times* for 10th June 1933, he states: 'Although there have been previous indications of electrical phenomena in the brain, general scientific opinion has been sceptical, the evidence not being clear enough. This was chiefly attributable to the relatively crude instrumental methods employed. Now the experimenters have succeeded in observing and instrumentally recording the electrical behaviour of the brain.'

the body, and especially is that the case when the sinuses are the part of the body concerned.

The philosopher who insists on getting at the basic root and cause of every effect, may be asked to explain *how* it is that we can make air movement backward and forward in the mouth as we wish. One gentleman replied that the air movement was caused by contraction of the abdominal muscles. To this theory I objected, but as he equally persisted, I altered my question and asked how we are able to change our point of activity to the mouth or nose as we wish. That, I said, could not possibly be traced to muscular control in the stomach. To this he was compelled to assent, and he acknowledged that we could only attribute the change simply to will power. That admission at once established the possibility of Sinus Tone Production, for the same will power which can effect a change of activity from the lower to the second level of air, can determine a change from the second to the upper level. Directly the air movement is made at the upper level silence is an impossibility for the air is moving in confined spaces.

A curious but very simple blunder made by every one of my critics is that of looking upon the vocal air column in the same light as they would regard a piano or a violin string. A piano string is in itself lifeless and cannot move without an extraneous energy. The air column in the body is *itself alive* and always in a state of movement and will so continue while life lasts. No outside influence is needed to set it in vibration. The short-sightedness of man has hitherto given the air column a choice of only two movements from the lungs, viz., out of the mouth or down the nose. Sinus theories have made the simple discovery that there is a third and very important means of breath exit, namely, from the sinuses and down the nose, a level which hitherto has not been consciously brought into activity. It is not so much a question of how do we set the air in movement to produce voice, but a question of shall we exhale our active breath from the level of *A*, *B*, *C*, or *D* (Figure 2). The levels *A* and *B* are obviously those which are in normal use, but those at *C* and *D* are inactive unless used for vocal purposes.

As the pianist knows that on his hands are five different points at which he can place activity in order to play his instrument so the vocalist, trained on Sinus principles, knows that he can control the air not only at *A*, *B*, *C*, and *D* but also at *E*, *F*, *G*, *H*.

How the will power is able to effect the movement, I am content to leave other people to discover if they can. It seems to me that the will can only act through an intermediary agent. For instance, a friend of mine was a very fine organist and pianist. In his later years he was afflicted with creeping paralysis; his will power and mentality were still brilliant, but not having the nerve power to control his muscles, the will power was useless for the purpose of playing. In any case the changing of the air movement at either of the four levels cannot be a muscular act and it is a matter of no practical importance whether the cause of the initial air movement is regarded as an electric current or more tentatively as a nerve impulse from the brain.[1] This may be left as a matter for research to those who have time and interest for the pursuit. For our present purpose it is sufficient to realize that the will has the power of creating an air movement at either of the four levels as may be desired. As we can control the air at the four levels *A*, *B*, *C*, *D*, Figure 2, it is not difficult to believe that the same control is possible in a horizontal plane on the level at *C*, between the frontal and the sphenoid sinuses.

The perfect control of the air and of every detail concerning it is a matter which must be experienced before it can be fully appreciated, but the reader may believe that the detailed rules which are to be given, only find a place here because it has been fully proved that they are at the service of every student and would-be vocalist, and the utility of the rules is the sole reason for the existence of this book. In *Grove's Dictionary of Music* (1928 edition), Dr. Aikin in his article on *Singing* remarks, 'While the whole of humanity is probably in some measure acquainted with the feeling of a desire to sing, and the form and condition of the vocal instruments appear to be as a rule normally fitted for the production of musical sound, the wonder is that everybody cannot do it.' If it were understood that voice is formed in the sinuses at and above the eye level, then every one would be able to sing.

[1] Sir Arthur Keith believes that up to the present, man has made use of only 50 per cent. of his brain. Dr. Frederick Tilney, Professor of Neurology at Columbia University, takes a more extreme view and declares that we have made use of only one-fifth of it. It is not at the moment a very important matter which specialist gives the correct percentage, but it is certain that the Sinus theories of voice production will considerably lessen the latent tract.

One of my professional pupils told me that on an occasion a lad in a singing class came to him and asked to be excused attending as he was quite unable to control pitch, and at each school he had attended he had been turned out of the singing class. My pupil told the lad to wait until the class was over, and then, taking him alone, explained in detail so far as he thought necessary the facts of Sinus Tone Production. In five minutes the lad was able to sing a scale. I have had the same experience many times, but the fact that my pupils can thus produce results with their pupils shows that success does not depend upon the influence or smartness of any particular tutor, but rests upon simple and scientific truth.

The laws or rules which govern the Voice Beautiful are fortunately not numerous, and will make no serious demands on the student's memory, but they will require a keen ear on the part of the tutor, and a perception and skill, with remedies for bad tone, which will be a new experience to the vocal cord trainer. The rules are intended for the assistance of the ordinary mortal who desires to sing for sheer pleasure; as well as for the more ambitious person who desires to sing professionally. Yet even to the magnificent vocal genius, if we may judge from the many sudden failures which have been known, there comes the time when scientific rules for voice would be a veritable godsend.

The first, or perhaps we should say, one of the first points that the student of Sinus Tone Production has to realize is that singing not merely should be, but *must* be non-muscular so far as tone is concerned. Now let us examine this apparently simple statement. We already know by experience, perhaps bitter experience, that orthodox vocal cord training demands a control of the larynx either high or low according to the individual idea of the tutor.[1] Then the tongue needs adjusting.[2] The ribs also demand attention.[3] Miss Liza Lehmann urges the importance of raising the uvula,[4] and Mlle. Marchesi the necessity of holding the glottis contracted.[5] This by no means exhausts the anatomical and muscular directions given for the assistance of the vocal

[1] *Musical Times*, May and September 1928.

[2] *How to Sing*, by Lilli Lehmann. Published by the Macmillan Co.

[3] *Jean de Reszke*. Published by Gerald Howe.

[4] *Practical Hints for the Students of Singing*. Published by The Epworth Press.

[5] *Singer's Pilgrimage*. Published by Grant Richards.

student by people of acknowledged reputation. But even these few are likely to prove of sufficient difficulty to keep the vocalist well occupied. He (or she) will start by getting the larynx into the highest (or lowest) possible position, then groove the tongue (or flatten it), after this expand the ribs at the waist line—of course keeping the larynx and tongue in the correct position (whatever it may be)—and then with the uvula well raised, the glottis contracted and the floating ribs 'trained to act as bellows,'[1] he is ready to start singing by allowing a 'large force of outrushing air to distend the rings of his windpipe.'[2] What a programme! but it is on orthodox and accepted lines.

Sinus Tone Production in the place of all these paraphernalia relies on the one accomplishment of mental control of a column of moving air. There must not be *one* conscious muscular movement, and further there is no need for any additional conscious movement than that which we make whilst we sit in a chair with our hands gently folded. When we hold in our hand a pen, there is the weight of that pen to uphold. If we reduce the weight of the pen to the weight of a feather, we are still actively employed in supporting that feather weight, negligible though it may be. When we sing we merely set in movement the air in our sinuses instead of the air in the mouth or nose. This implies no extra work and no more physical exertion than is implied in the action of the heart beating, and this complete absence of muscular movement should be the first detail to which the attention of both tutor and pupil is directed. This is the 'very simple need' of the vocalist, and so I conform to the dictum that 'nearly all pioneers for the most part utter a very simple truth.'[3] One must, however, realize that neither the simplicity of a theory nor the sincerity of its author is any guarantee of truth. Let us therefore endeavour to balance the pros and the cons, and so determine the correct reasoning which will give us the delight which Francis Bacon had in his mind when he wrote, 'No pleasure is comparable to the standing upon the vantage ground of Truth.' The question is whether that 'vantage ground' lies within the domain of muscular work with respect to voice or of non-muscular work. Which from the purely theoretical standpoint is the more probable?

[1] Melba.

[2] *Scientific Tone Production*, by Miss Mary James. Published by the Boston Music Co.

[3] Richard King.

Do we have to adjust our anatomy before listening? No, our anatomical conditions are by nature ready for the reception of sound. If whilst taking a walk we meet a friend, do we make careful preparations of ribs and uvula, before we say, 'Well, Jack, I am pleased to see you'? The nose also needs no special preparation in order to appreciate the perfume of the violet. Within certain limits such as the use of lenses to correct astigmatism, short or long sight, and so on, a similar line of thought is applicable to the eyes; that is to say, we do not have to make conscious muscular adjustments for the use of our eyes when we want to read a book. Why then should all this extraordinary displacement of natural conditions be necessary or even advisable when we want to sing?

Robert Schumann, in a laudable but fatal endeavour to improve the muscular conditions which the Almighty arranged for our hands, rendered the third finger of his right hand useless, and so ruined his cherished ambition of becoming a first-rate pianist. Many are the pupils who have come to me for training and have explained to me that they have spent hours before the mirror trying to raise the uvula. To these people I have always had just one reply: 'If God had intended the uvula to be in a high position, He would not have left it in a low one.' Why spend hours of your time in a stupid endeavour to alter a perfectly natural arrangement of nature? This is only the negative side of the matter. The positive will be found on page 51, where we shall see the reason for its natural position, and I trust come to the conclusion that after all GOD does know better than man the correct position for the uvula, as well as for the other members of our anatomy. Then as regards Madame Melba's instruction to 'train the floating ribs to act as bellows,' I think possibly the best way to deal with this detail will be to give an account of a conversation I had some years ago with the late Dr. Tom Haigh. We met at Oxford, and in his cheery manner he said to me, 'Well, Mr. White, how goes the work?' 'Thank you,' I replied, 'very well indeed.' 'Of course,' he went on, 'you must admit that for years past all our best tutors have been teaching their pupils to direct the breath from the lungs to the head.' 'Yes,' I said, 'but that is just what I do not do. I teach my pupils to direct the breath from the head downwards.' 'Yes,' he argued, 'but you must start at the lungs before you can get an air movement in the head.' 'No,' I said, 'the start is from the head downwards.' 'Do not fuss,' said he, 'the starting place must be the lungs.' 'My dear sir,' said I emphatically and slowly, 'if the air in the head is moved downwards, no power in the world can prevent the air which is in the lungs moving upwards and taking its place.' Dr. Haigh looked very thoughtful for a minute or two and then said, 'Mr. White, that is very wonderful.' I said, 'It *is* wonderful.' I can quite believe that many readers will not see anything 'wonderful' in the altered conception of the air or breath movement. Dr. Haigh, however, had previously devoted some time to the consideration of Sinus work, and he saw that the change would entail an alteration which would indeed be wonderful. And he was right. For it entirely does away with the idea of the ribs acting as bellows for the breath. Neither pushing nor energy is required for a downward movement. The student merely *wills* the air to move from the sinuses. On orthodox lines there is an upward movement of air from a low position to a higher; in Sinus work there is a downward movement from a high position to a lower. The former of necessity entails a pushing action, and possibly a thrusting one, which is always wrong.[1] By starting the air from the sinuses downwards, the vocalist not only eliminates all pushing, but he gets clear of all muscular movement for tone production, for the simple reason that there are not any muscles connected with the bones of the head above the hard palate. By giving us no movable parts in the skull, nature has enabled us—if we only knew it—to sing with the greatest possible freedom and ease. Thus Dr. Haigh was correct when he said, 'That is very wonderful.'

A parallel may be found in the study of the growth of trees. In all trees there are delicate pipes, as tiny as hairs, known as capillary tubes, which extend from the roots, up the stem to the leaves. There is a continuous series of them from the roots which draw the water from the soil, whence it travels along the pipes to the leaves. There the water is used in making sugar and some also evaporates into the air in what is called transpiration. When some of the water is used up or lost in the leaves, more water *must* rise to take its place. Similarly when air in the head has been used for tone making, the air from the lungs *must* rise and take its place. This to some readers might perhaps seem

[1] *Science and Singing*, page 37.

quite obvious, but this way of Dame Nature is unfortunately not taken into account by the orthodox writer on vocal matters. One writes of the vocal cords as being ' two elastic bands, inside the larynx, kept in tension . . . so that they can be put in vibration by the *blast* of air *pushed* by the lungs.'[1] Another writes of the vocalist raising a ' sufficient pressure of air in his chest and windpipe to *force* open the vocal cords by means of a *blast* of air.'[2] A third says similarly : ' We, perhaps, should have referred before to another element in the tensing of the vocal cords, viz., that furnished by the blast of air. . . . To raise the pitch the expiratory blast must be increased, for as we have seen, the pitch of the tone depends upon the strength of the expiratory pressure.'[3] Our vocal tutors will have learned an important lesson when they realize the fact, that as air leaves the mouth or nose either in a state of tonal vibration as voice, or without tonal vibration in silence, so air from the lungs *must* take its place, just as moisture *must* rise to the leaves of the tree from the root during transpiration. No pressure of any kind is needed, much less a *blast* of air.

The full value of the downward air movement can be understood only by properly testing it. As I have previously suggested,[4] it might help the student to look upon singing as *negative* work. I have also found it convenient and useful to describe the process as a ' metaphysical ' one to impress on pupils the fact that vocal tone must be produced by mental control alone. The real difficulty of fine singing is the creating an air movement in the sinuses without either making or permitting any muscular movement. Sir Joshua Reynolds once said that a picture must not only be done well, it must seem to have been done easily. The same applies to the performance of music. ' The laboured look is too often a sign-manual of the second-rate.'

Concerning singing, *blasts* of air should neither be written nor talked about, but the required air movement for tonal production must be completely independent of any conscious muscular movement. The organist has to work hard in order to get

[1] Dr. Marafioti.

[2] *The Singing Voice* by E. Garnett Passe. Published by Sir Isaac Pitman & Sons.

[3] *Voice Building and Tone Placing*, by Holbrook Curtis, M.D., page 42. Published by J. Curwen & Sons.

[4] *Science and Singing*, page 50 *b*.

independence between his hands and feet. I have read that Sir Edwin Landseer was able to make one drawing with his right hand whilst he made another with his left. Such is the freedom and independence which the tutor of Sinus Tone Production must teach his singing pupil, and that is the control for which the student must watch. In *The Melba Method* the first sentence is: 'It is easy to sing well and very difficult to sing badly.' In order to attempt an explanation of this apparent paradox the authoress continues, 'Let me say the same thing in other words. "In order to sing well it is necessary to sing easily."' Then we naturally wonder how it was that Madame Melba found it so 'easy to sing well.' The explanation is that she had not the tendency which most people have, to create muscular movements either in the throat or elsewhere whilst singing. Thus she had the utmost freedom of air movement.

'Nearly two hundred years ago Maupertuis tried to show that the principle of least action was one which but exhibited the wisdom of the Creator.'[1] This same principle, sometimes termed the principle of minimum energy, is extensively used by engineers in aeronautical work for building both aeroplanes and rigid airships. The principle applies in many respects in nature, and the sooner its application is directed to the study of singing so much the better will it be both for the art and for those who practise it.

There is a story that Michael Angelo once accepted from a gentleman an order for a statue. After a few months he paid a visit to the sculptor in order to see how the work was progressing. He was satisfied and was told he might call again in three months' time. This he did, and the artist explained that since the previous visit, one curve had been lessened, another had been increased, another part had been made slightly more prominent, whilst another had been a little levelled. 'Yes,' said the gentleman, 'I observe these trifles, but have you done nothing more?' 'No,' said Michael Angelo, 'I have not. It is trifles that make perfection, and perfection is no trifle.'

The next 'trifles,' then, concerning Sinus work deal again with air movement. We have seen that good vocal tone is created by a controlled air movement in the different sinuses, the pitch

[1] Dr. I. W. Mellow, in *Higher Mathematics for Students of Chemistry and Physics.*

being determined by the proportion of work allotted to the frontal sinuses, the anterior and posterior ethmoid cells and the sphenoid sinuses respectively. Further we have learnt the necessity for a downward movement from the sinuses, in distinction to an upward movement towards them. There remain three other details, ' trifles ' to those unacquainted with Sinus work, each of which is capable, if neglected, of ruining good tone, but if understood will play its part in producing the Voice Beautiful.

The first is the acoustic law that the higher the note the smaller must be the column of air which is used. As this matter has had much consideration in the previous two books,[1] it will require little argument here. It will suffice to say that the usual rule : ' In taking higher notes of course one must open the mouth a little wider,'[2] has no foundation save that of custom, and the custom is clearly contrary to the known laws of nature. Those who have learned to produce high notes with a very small mouth opening, have no desire to do the opposite, for they realize that the more open mouth entails increased energy and less beautiful tone.

The second and third details concerning air movement in tone production have so far been used only in my private practice and in the practice of those of my pupils who are teachers also. They are therefore published now for the first time. Before I attempt to explain them I want to stress the fact that they are founded on science and not merely on my personal opinions. My work in the realm of music has been to raise singing to the dignity of a science, working on reliable laws, and this in no way diminishes its value as an art, but on the contrary gives a sure and trustworthy means of presenting the art. Now, in the words of Dr. Whitehead, ' There can be no living science unless there is a widespread instinctive conviction of the existence of an *order of things*, and in particular of an order of nature.' It was indeed the study of a book entitled *Design in Nature*[3] which first gave me the idea which I describe now as the second detail in the science of Sinus Tone Production. The point which is brought out in *Design in Nature* is the ubiquity of the spiral form in nature's growth and movements. As I reflected upon this and studied

[1] *Science and Singing*, page 30. *Light on the Voice Beautiful*, page 83.
[2] Dr. Voorhees.
[3] By Dr. Pettigrew. Published by Longmans, Green & Co.

Dr. Pettigrew's numerous examples it became clear to me at last that another fresh truth could be added to the deuteronomy of the vocalist. 'The inorganic and organic kingdoms,' he writes, 'are constructed on similar lines.' They are not opposed to each other. On the contrary, they are interdependent, complemented, co-ordinated and conditioned. They are made for each other. No marvel, then, if plants and animals assume shapes and movements which are common in the heavenly bodies. (I append photographs of marvellous nebular arrangements. These arrangements are extremely suggestive in their bearing on movements in general, and on the movements in plants and animals in particular.)[1] If proof were wanting of the intimate relations subsisting between the inorganic kingdoms, and of the unity of plan which pervades all nature, these remarkable coincidences in spiral formations are well calculated to supply it. The inorganic and organic spirals cannot, everything considered, be regarded as chance productions. They undoubtedly owe their origin to the operation of a common law, and afford a striking proof of a First Cause.

Following on this line of thought, we arrive at what seems to me one of the most striking and wonderful harmonies of Sinus theories, namely, that they work in accordance with a universal law which dominates the universe.

The planets, revolving on their own axis and circling around the sun, are in attunement with the description given by the electron theory of matter, of electrons circling round a nucleus in every atom. Here in vocalism we have the central point of electric power emanating from the grey matter of the brain, and the air in the sinuses circling around that point. Seeing how universal is the law of spiral movement in nature, it seems certain that the air in the sinuses moving downwards must always take a spiral direction, similar to the thread of a screw, and starting from the highest point of the sinus. The practical value of this concept has proved astonishing to those who have learned how to use it.

This then is the second law for the control of air movement, namely, that the air must flow downwards with a spiral movement. There are two special advantages in carrying out this law.

[1] These spiral nebulae are the most remote objects known. Figure 3 shows a spiral nebula with the centre formed of stars and several stars showing through the nebula. It is only in the nearest spirals that individual stars can be seen, and these individual stars are each hundreds and thousands of times brighter than our sun. See Appendix VI.

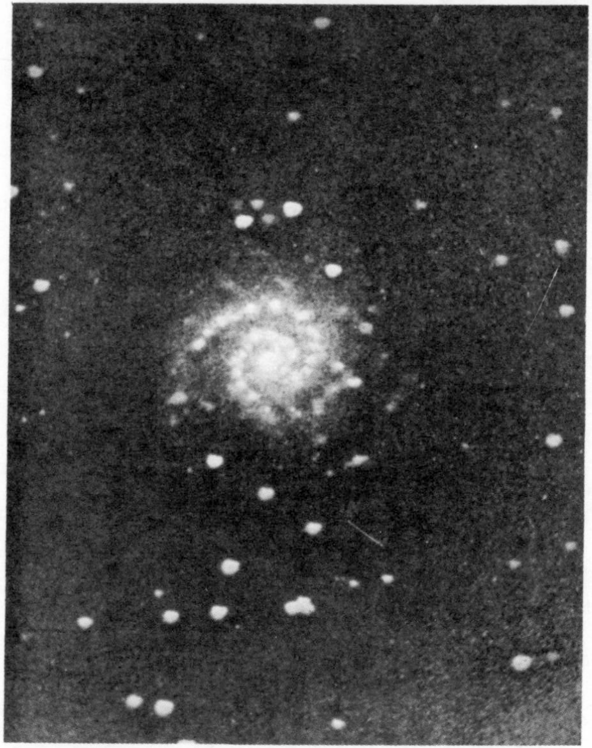

Figure 3. A Beautiful Right-handed Spiral Nebula

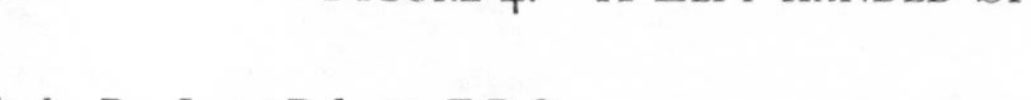

Figure 4. A Left-handed Spiral Nebula

Photographs by Dr. Isaac Roberts, F.R.S.

(*a*) It makes it easier to acquire the correct downward movement as opposed to a forward movement of air.[1] (*b*) The spiral movement of the air enables the vocalist to sing quite long phrases with an ease which astonishes the uninitiated. It is obvious that the air having this movement is available for longer use than if it moved in a straight line. The absolute control which every one has in this apparently small ' trifle ' is undoubtedly remarkable. I will give an instance. A child of about twelve years of age was having singing lessons in order to improve a very poor voice. At one of her early lessons I noticed her tone was forced and rather hard. I therefore stopped her and said, ' You know that when you have finished your bath and the water is allowed to run down the waste pipe, it does not leave the bath moving in a straight line, but it circles round and round.' ' Yes,' she replied, ' I have seen it.' ' Well,' I answered, ' that is just the way the air leaves the little boxes in your head. If you will *think* of the air circling in that way, you will get the correct tone.' She at once succeeded in getting a really beautiful vocal tone. It is one of the details which ensure the creation of tone which is beautiful. It is probable that had the same direction been given to an adult the result might have been less instantaneous, for the questions, *How* ? *Why* ? would have rushed into the mentality of the pupil, but the child, acting with the simplicity and faith of a child, at once produced the required result.[2]

Students of Sinus Tone Production know that good vocal tone is caused in the first place by a correct blending of air movement from the various sinuses ; the more acute the pitch the more the frontal sinus is used, and the deeper the note so much more the sphenoid sinus is used. By examining Figure 2 it will be seen that the air from the frontal sinus must have a backward as well as a downward movement. Thus for a tenor or soprano to produce a good quality note beyond *or* a forward position is wanted, with a downward and *backward* movement from that position. This then forms the third

[1] This matter is further considered on page 76 of *Science and Singing*.

[2] It is a matter of interest that this law of circling air is in harmony with the phrase used by many Italian vocal tutors, *Bisogna filare la voce*. Their idea was correct, but unfortunately for the pupil, it was hardly possible to give practical directions for carrying out the principle, because vocal cord production predicates muscular tension and activity wrongly located.

detail already mentioned. Again let me give an illustration. A tenor pupil brought me a song in which the final bars were

a - lone

He said, ' I can sing the whole of this song excepting the last note, which will crack!' I asked him to sing the last verse of the song, and it went very well until he reached the final word, and then the G suddenly disappeared. I showed him Figure 6 in *Science and Singing* and explained the air movement. When I felt he understood the technique of the matter, I said ' Now let us try, but you must not on any account think of getting the G, neither must you attempt to *do* anything, but your mind must be definitely concentrated on willing the air which is at the point D [Figure 2, page 30] to move quickly backwards and downwards from that point. By so doing you will be concentrating on the air movement which will produce G, instead of merely the wish to get G without knowing how.' He immediately produced the required sound with excellent tone and perfect ease !

So the three laws referred to on page 41 may be summarized as follows :

1. In producing vocal tone the air must be allowed to make a circling movement in a downward direction.

2. The higher the note required, the smaller must be the air column for producing that note.

3. In producing high notes the air movement must be *from* a forward point, backwards and downwards.

I can quite hear my sceptical brethren saying with disdain, ' Thank you, I want to be an artist, and give a poetical rendering of the words of my song, so that I may thrill my audience with the glory of the music. Such work will make me only a mechanic.' The last eight words reveal persistent misunderstanding. The vocal student of Sinus theories has to study vocal technique as a scientific subject, realizing what are the mechanical means which will produce the tone he wants. When this mechanical education has made progress, then the tutor supplies a song which will test how far the pupil is able, as an artist, freely to carry out the rules he has studied in mechanics. Thus one enlarges on the programme already given : ' First the skill of the scientific mechanic, then the glorious artist, beautiful and free.'

One objection to the scientific approach to voice production has been advanced in the following terms : 'There is a science of voice—a very valuable and important science—but science deals primarily with quantity. Measurement is of the essence of science. In voice training the greatest thing you are dealing with is quality. You can praise quality, but never measure it.'[1] Superficially this seems a sound enough criticism, but after all measurement is not only a matter of feet and inches and cubic centimetres. In any work of art one of the factors contributing to its quality or beauty is the factor of proportion ; and proportion is capable of analysis in terms of measurement, whether or not the artist consciously so analyses it. Often enough intuitive artistic judgment must go hand in hand with a more concrete kind of measurement. If it were not so, how could we get the graceful outline of a noble cathedral ? And how could we get the magnificent organ in the cathedral, whose pipes have all been measured to an inch, nay to a quarter of an inch, whose glorious tones can be 'measured' only by the discerning ear and mind ?

We know that the vocal cords of a woman are half an inch in length, and with this half-inch she is supposed to create two, two and a half, or even three octaves of tone. It was the scientific impossibility of reconciling these two measurements which first led me to reject the vocal cord theory and to discover and propound the facts of Sinus Tone Production. Sinus vocal training thus conforms with scientific principles and *begins with measurement*. But more than this ; the ear of the tutor is engaged during each lesson in technique in assessing proportions : whether the right balance is being attained among the various sinuses ; whether the volume and shape of the moving air column is exactly proportioned to the note which is being produced, and so on. The vocal trainer has to estimate the perpendicular, horizontal and diametrical air movements which his pupil makes and further he must teach his pupil to listen with the same concentration. Very frequently a pupil will find it advantageous to close the eyes whilst studying technique in order to listen the more attentively to the tone which he is producing and to notice its position. It is impossible to express in writing the exact quality of tone which indicates the amount of movement from one position to another. Some elementary pupils in changing from one note to another of a different pitch begin by making too big

[1] Mr. Field-Hyde.

a horizontal movement, whilst others will make the movement too small. Nearly all beginners in starting a note fail to get the right position in a vertical direction, for their activity is usually placed at a spot that is too low. As a general rule the endeavour of the tutor should be to get vocal tone from the most forward position that is then possible in the head. When that particular position has been used for some weeks, or possibly months, a new position further forward will develop giving a note beyond that which was created by the previous position. With further work another position will become available giving again a different note, and so this shifting of position continues until the most forward position in the frontal sinus has been reached, with of course a corresponding addition to the vocal compass of the student. One result of this process, and a very notable one, is the feeling of enlargement in the vocal instrument experienced by fully trained Sinus students. This spaciousness gives them that freedom and ease which is so noticeable. In the early lessons the tutor must explain this idea of distance, when the student is practising an upward interval of a fourth or more. The vocal cord singer is fixed, consciously or unconsciously, to the one spot in his throat, and it is often therefore a surprise to the student to find what extensive changes in position he can and must make in singing the various intervals. It cannot be too strongly urged that on Sinus principles the whole mental conception of voice must be re-set. The half-inch of a woman's vocal cord represents the size of the vocal machine on orthodox lines. It has been argued that the sinuses are too small to act as a musical instrument. The foolishness of such a statement is obvious when we consider that the frontal sinuses only would easily hold twenty-five pairs of vocal cords, and the whole of the head cavities would probably accommodate 150 pairs of vocal cords. Thus we see the immensely increased area that we possess for the purpose of voice production under Sinus principles. The singer must not think of his head in the terms of the number of inches required for his hat, but as a vocal machine 150 times bigger than vocal cord teaching had allowed him to believe. Such a mental attitude opens up freedom and vocal possibilities which have never before been visualized. When these matters have been understood and brought under control or nearly so, the tutor may direct the pupil's attention to the development of power in the voice, which is carried out by blending the anterior and posterior ethmoid cells, and the sphenoid sinus, with the frontal sinus. The person without practical experience quite naturally wonders *how* all this is to be done. The only answer that can be given here is: 'With the assistance of a competent and experienced tutor, and with persevering practice.' The reader, however, may rest assured that the work is perfectly definite and certain in its results.

In the art of Sinus Tone Production a sense of willingness and perseverance in the pupil are the only two qualifications demanded by the tutor. The *real work* of getting a voice of beauty rests entirely with the master, providing the pupil has the aforesaid qualifications. If the quality of the voice does not improve, then the ear or the judgment of the tutor is at fault in giving wrong directions to his pupil, in fact his *measurements* have proved incorrect. And how delicate and sensitive those measurements are! There was a time years ago when I began to question myself as to whether I was becoming too fussy with pupils in expecting and working for these fine gradations of tone both in quality and volume. I was still wondering when one day I read of a ruling machine that could on the edge, that is to say the thickness of this leaf, rule fourteen parallel lines. That at once settled the matter, for, I said to myself, if it be possible to make a metal machine capable of such delicate work, it is quite certain that the vocal machine which GOD gave to me is not less sensitive, and from that day forward my pupils and I worked for an even greater precision in tone quality, tone placing and air movement than we had previously contemplated, and our attempts were successful. Moreover to the artist who loves his work and would scorn to produce something inferior, there was the added joy of discovering that the voice which already was very good was capable of being made even better, and so further triumphs could be won and greater difficulties conquered.

The delicacy of the mechanical control is the means which leads to the ultimate perfection of the artist. Probably one of the most interesting and precise instruments for measurement is the Fabry-Perot interferometer, by which it is possible to record with accuracy the millionth part of an inch. Measurements for dealing with human sight have already been brought to a similar point of perfection, and the art of Sinus Tone Production brings the human voice into the same category, and gives the vocalist that perennial source of delight to every artist, namely, the consciousness of thorough mastery of every detail of his subject. Thus it is clear that anyone who speaks of the impossibility of applying measurement to voice is overlooking the beautiful precision of movement which is possible in Sinus work.

'Medicine in the third quarter of the eighteenth century was but just beginning not to resent the intrusion of the infant sciences upon tradition; now it is based on science through and through and is less than nothing without it.'[1] It is admittedly impossible for the orthodox tutor to include voice within the circle of a definite and exact science even after 1,700 years of throat study and examination, but I venture to prophesy that before many years have passed, journalists will be writing of singing on similar lines to the medical survey just quoted, and will state that it was not until the twentieth century that science was allowed to intrude upon vocal tradition, and will admit that singing 'is less than nothing without it.'

Before such a high standard can be attained in vocal science the pupil must realize that the study of the mechanic is a separate matter from the study of the artist. In order to impress and fix in the minds of those students who are in the early stages of training the importance of this fundamental idea of mechanics, I sometimes turn suddenly to a pupil and say, 'You know you have not come here to learn singing.' This, of course, always causes surprise and the person at once wonders why he or she has come. So I continue, 'Do you know why you are here?' The usual reply is, 'I thought I had come to learn singing'; to which I answer, 'No, you have come to learn the *control of the machine* which creates singing.' This is an idea which is novel to every pupil.

To be taught the art of singing was the one ambition which filled the mind of the student when starting his artistic career. He anticipated lessons in dramatic interpretation, enunciation, deportment, and let us not forget breathing! How indeed would the average singing master earn his fee, if he did not give lessons on breathing? Enunciation, interpretation, deportment are subjects which have their full share of attention in the curriculum of Sinus training and the artistic side is never forgotten, but a full control of the vocal machine is the first detail for the student's

[1] *Daily Telegraph*, 17th May 1923.

work. He may, according to his ability be asked at his first practical lesson to sing an octave,

or five notes,

or two notes,

or even one note,

but during the lesson he must be shown how his vocal machine can be controlled so that the note or series of notes may be of a beautiful quality, or in the case of a very harsh voice of such a character that it will at all events develop into a beautiful quality. The scholar having come to the master for tuition, it is the definite work and duty of the tutor to see that his pupil makes the first step towards that direct control of the vocal machine which results in the production of beautiful tone.

> The process of learning an art should, even in the case of those who have the finest natural endowment for it, be more conscious than its practice. Mr. Harry Vardon, when he is acquiring a new grip, is wise to make himself more conscious of the relation between his will and his wrists than when he is addressing himself to his approach-shot, at the decisive hole of a championship.[1]

So, the first ' stage of control ' for the Sinus student is to find for a given note a correct position and a correct air movement from it. By degrees and with patient and watchful practice, the varying positions for the varying notes in the vocal compass become thoroughly established. The violinist has to spend years in learning the technique of a correct finger placement. The organist has to spend years in gaining a proper foot technique and the flautist must develop an unerring lip technique, and the scientific vocalist must spend years of work in order to develop a perfect Sinus technique. Is it worth while ? Well, that is a question which each individual must answer for himself. If people knew for a certainty that the work and study would produce a voice of beauty, as well as tremendous health benefits (which we consider in the next

[1] *The Art of Thought*, by Graham Wallas, Emeritus Professor of Political Science at London University. Published by Jonathan Cape, Ltd.

chapter), then there would probably be few lovers of music who would refuse time and care for the purpose.

Let us now consider another detail of the vocal machine which has so far eluded all attempts to find a useful place or to get assigned to it any work in the human body. I refer to the uvula. From the outlook adopted by vocal teachers concerning this appendage, one would imagine that nature had made a great mistake in entrusting to us this small cylindrical body, for it is invariably made an urgent rule that the pupil shall try and raise the soft palate to the utmost extent and thus get the uvula out of the way so far as is possible. Under the limelight of Sinus vocal principles, it will be shown that the uvula is not ' one of Nature's agreeable blunders.' Let us take the advice of William Wordsworth :

> Come forth into the light of things,
> Let Nature be your teacher.

' Design in Nature ' is indeed a thoroughly enthralling study, and the intimate relations between structure and function cannot be overstressed. So far as vocal cord theories are concerned no such relationship has ever been discovered. This is obvious from the fact that the high priests who rule over the vocal universe have not even settled among themselves whether the human voice belongs to the violin, the reed or the siren family. The only use they can find for the uvula is that it keeps the student out of mischief by making him spend hours in the endeavour to get it out of the way. In Sinus principles the structural relationship of voice is evident at every point. It is seen in the perfectly marvellous adjustments of the hard and soft palates in the mouth. The vibrating air leaving the sinuses will strike directly on to the hard palate, which forms an ideal resonator and will convey the air vibrations to the air below it, in the mouth. That detail has already had consideration, so we pass on to the soft palate.

Dr. Voorhees, in commenting on the soft palate, states that ' the function of the soft palate in singing has been much disputed and bandied about in teachers' discussions, and there is still no unanimity of opinion among them concerning this matter in so far as I am aware.' The statement is correct, but it is worthy of note that the doctor makes no attempt to throw any light on the dispute, and we can only conclude that he is unable to do so, for the medical profession is no more definite in its views on the matter than the musical. Sinus theories explain the anatomical and the artistic meaning of the disputed enigma, as they have also explained other knotty and puzzling questions. They give rise, indeed, to a situation

> Where order in variety we see
> And where, though all things differ, all agree.[1]

We have already seen the great importance and the universal predominance of the spiral form and movement in all nature. The design of the soft palate gives us yet a further example. We may take it for granted that it is generally known that the soft palate forms two arches with the uvula dropping in the centre between them thus: We have already seen that it would be contrary to all design in nature that we should have the roof of the mouth in a straight line as from *D* to *E*; a straight line being barred from nature's concept, the alternative would be an arch upwards as at *A C B*,

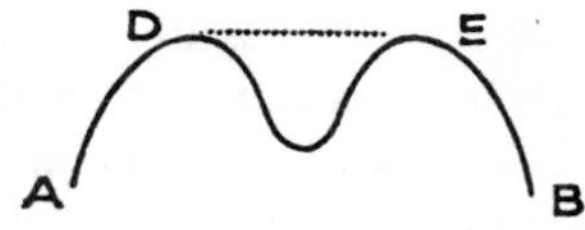

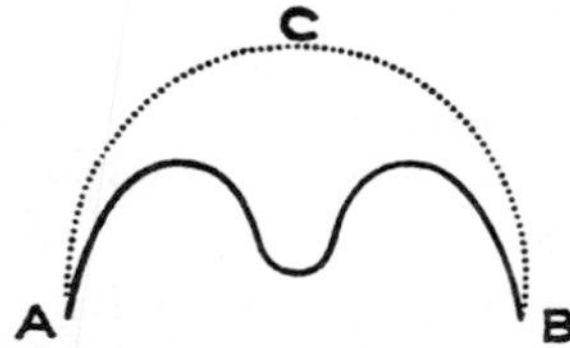

This means that if the uvula were absent, the air which is coming up the windpipe and passing into the head for the creation of tone in the sinuses would be exposed to the varying air movements created in the mouth when consonant sounds are produced and serious irregularities in the tonal air column would result. The uvula therefore acts as a shield to allow a smooth and even current of air to pass into the head cavities, and provides yet another example of the perfect ordering of nature. The practical effect of endeavouring to raise the soft palate in singing is to leave quite unprotected that frail breath column which the vocal cords have just previously shaped compactly and directed towards the sinuses. By pointing the lips and drawing them together—as if one were about to blow out a candle—the points *A* and *B*, that is to say the soft palate on either side of the uvula, can be drawn towards the uvula and so nearly shut off the air in the mouth from the air current behind the uvula which is *on its way* to tonal production. The following practical experience illustrates the importance of this

[1] Alexander Pope.

matter. A pupil was taking the name part in the opera *The Student Prince.*[1] In the following phrase,

he found it very difficult to get the high note on *we* with good tone. I therefore asked him to take the three minims on the *wa* of *waltz*. This he accomplished quite easily. I then explained to him that the *tz* of *waltz* and the consonant of *we*, each produced a forward directional air movement through the mouth, and in so doing interfered with the air current passing into the head cavities. Having realized this fact, he minimized the *tz* and *w*, and was successful in producing an excellent G, because the air current was not damaged.

Here is yet another link in the chain of evidence for the truth of Sinus theories. To those—and they are now a goodly number—who take the trouble to weigh the evidence for and against the new theory, it is a matter of delight and surprise to observe the mechanical perfection of the vocal apparatus.[2]

> Nature never did betray
> The heart that loved her. 'Tis her privilege,
> Through all the years of this our life, to lead
> From joy to joy.[3]

The vocal cord student has no experience of the joy of studying the whole of the vocal machine from the diaphragm to the brain and discovering with what microscopic perfection the anatomy in all its minutiae is designed for the use of the vocalist. Every detail of the vocal cords, their length, shape, texture and position testify to their inability to act as sound producers, but indicate their marvellous beauty of design as breath controllers.[4] The various sinuses, maxillary, sphenoid, and frontal, together with the posterior and anterior cells which had never been mentioned in any vocal work previous to the publication of *Science and Singing* in 1909 (nor had any medical or scientific work ever assigned to them any definite utility in the economy of nature), now assume a most important role both from a health and an

[1] By Sigmund Romberg.
[2] See Appendix VII.
[3] Wordsworth.
[4] *Science and Singing*, page 53.

artistic point of view. The air they contain has been proved by the Sinus tutor and Sinus student to be under absolute control.

The process of securing that control and developing the voice is at once mental and physical, illustrating indeed the intimate relationship between mind and body. Because the study of the throat, with photographs or figures, *ad nauseam*, of vocal cords, and thyroid, arytenoid and cricoid cartilages, has never improved a voice nor made a singer, the orthodox vocal world has been tempted to conclude that 'not one of the vocal problems confronting the vocal student is physical.' But the orthodox have never studied the osseous construction of the head as a vocal machine. The singer's problems are certainly not solved by physical means if by that is implied the muscular manipulation of the throat, because the throat is not the part of the vocal machine which creates tone. But every vocal problem confronting the student, although not muscular, is physical, in the sense that beautiful tone depends upon the correct use of the air in different sinuses and knowledge of the physical condition and position of the sinuses is invaluable to the vocalist. In this sense singing is physical because the physical conditions have to be controlled—but by mental and not muscular means; and with careful and thoughtful practice the singer and speaker can gain as much technique and definite control over his vocal machine as Kreisler has over his violin. But it is impossible to emphasize too much the fact that the control is an acoustic, that is to say an air control, centred from the brain to the various cavities which are below it.

So important is this that every new pupil, seated in a comfortable arm-chair, starts his technical training with me so placed that I can keep a watchful eye on the student, without making him feel too conscious that I am doing so. The exercise would probably be from either the mediant or the dominant to the tonic. Invariably a preparatory mouth movement is made together with an inhalation. Directly my eye catches these movements, I stop the pupil before even a single note has been sung, and point out that there must be no activity around the mouth; air movement in a downward direction from the sinuses being the only activity either required or permitted. There are very few who realize how difficult this is,[1] and the more so, as the mouth movements are

[1] See pages 29*a*, 49 and 103

frequently very slight and quite unconscious on the part of the student. Almost, though perhaps not quite, as difficult is it, in the early stages of training to avoid taking a breath in preparation for singing. Moreover it is always a great astonishment to the pupil to be forbidden to do so. The exclamation usually is, 'But I must breathe!', with which great thought I agree, but point out to my pupil and critic, that when he reached home he would hardly expect his sister or father to take the biggest possible breath in order to ask him, 'Did you enjoy your lesson?', and in like manner he would not fill his lungs to their utmost capacity in order to answer, 'Yes, I did.' The pupil of course sees the absurdity of acting in the manner described, and some faint glimmer of 'Light on the Voice Beautiful' begins to dawn on his mind and intelligence. I then proceed to explain that the first step in learning to sing, is the setting into movement a tiny column of air without permitting any physical or muscular movement however small; that is to say, the air is to move by the will of the pupil, but the pupil is not to move. Necessarily this produces a very small tone, but if the air movement is properly initiated and controlled, the tone though tiny is free and beautiful, and from that perfect freedom development towards power begins, and so the acorn becomes the oak tree and the oak tree becomes a forest of beauty and strength. This is a matter which should be explained to every pupil, that the beauty through sheer freedom develops into strength. Knowing the noisy and sometimes even howling sounds which too frequently come from vocal studios, it is quite natural that the beginner should in his mind, even if not by word of mouth, question the utility of such apparently feeble notes, especially as that particular quality of voice is generally known by the foolish term, falsetto.[1] So in order to avoid any misconception I explain that the tiny sound is the result of the smallest possible air movement from just one cavity only, without bringing into use other sinuses as harmonics, or the maxillary sinuses as resonators. Further, under these conditions the diploe all round the skull is also inactive as a resonator. When the purity and smoothness of the tone are absolutely assured, then, and not before, is the time to think of developing power.

The fact that voice does develop in both beauty and power with such training is attested in a remarkable manner

[1] *Science and Singing*, page 51.

by W. Graham Robertson in his delightful volume, *Time Was*.[1] He is writing of Madame Sarah Bernhardt and concerning her voice he says :

> It was the cooing of doves, the running of streams, the falling of soft spring rain. And its carrying power!
>
> I remember calling at the stage door of some theatre in London to leave a message and asking the door-keeper whether the act was finished or if Madame Sarah was still on the stage. The man merely said, 'Listen.' I listened, and up from the far distant stage and along passages, and up stairways, through heavy swing doors, came the murmuring chant of the *voix d'or*. No other voice was audible ; when the voice of Sarah ceased there was silence till it began again. 'Rum, ain't it ?' commented the stage door-keeper.

And what was the clue to the mystery ? In this case it was *not* a naturally well-placed voice, for in her youth her voice was easily exhausted.

> Sarah Bernhardt herself told me that she had hit upon the false voice as a means of saving her natural voice ; that she achieved it by pitching the voice up in the head and *producing it through the nose*, and that, by alternating it with her natural utterance, she could come safely through long tirades which otherwise would have left her speechless.

Before 1880 Sarah Bernhardt had discovered by sheer intuition, and without any knowledge of science or anatomy, the great value of the so-called falsetto voice, or, to write more correctly, the value of the frontal sinus position of voice.

In 1909, that is twenty-two years before the publication of *Time Was*, *Science and Singing*, the first treatise on Sinus vocal theories, was published, treating from a scientific point of view the discovery which Sarah Bernhardt 'hit upon.'

Necessarily the development of voice from a pure falsetto to full tone and power demands very considerable care and watchfulness on the part of both the tutor and pupil, but especially the tutor, because he has to hear and detect wrong movements and wrong tone of which the pupil has no knowledge. The first attempt to get a *crescendo* from a small note should be made at a pitch which is about the middle of the pupil's compass. The tendency of the pupil will invariably be to increase the tone from the sphenoid sinus only, thereby producing a hard and harsh

[1] Published by Hamish Hamilton, Ltd. I am much indebted to Mr. Robertson for his kind permission to make these quotations.

quality. Then it is the duty of the tutor to explain that a note like for a *mezzo* voice, produced *pp* from the frontal sinus, must keep that particular quality of tone going, and get the *crescendo* by gradually bringing into action the anterior and the posterior ethmoid cells and the sphenoid sinus, and the experience of the master detects whether this action is being properly controlled. In all probability the student will begin by making a physical push or exertion to create the louder tone. This also must be stopped instantly, and the pupil shown that physical exertion is as unnecessary for a loud note as it is for a soft one, for the physical or anatomical explanation of a loud note is, that the vocal cords come further apart and so allow a bigger column of air to come into action. The correct sensation therefore for a *crescendo* is a feeling of expansion, but never a

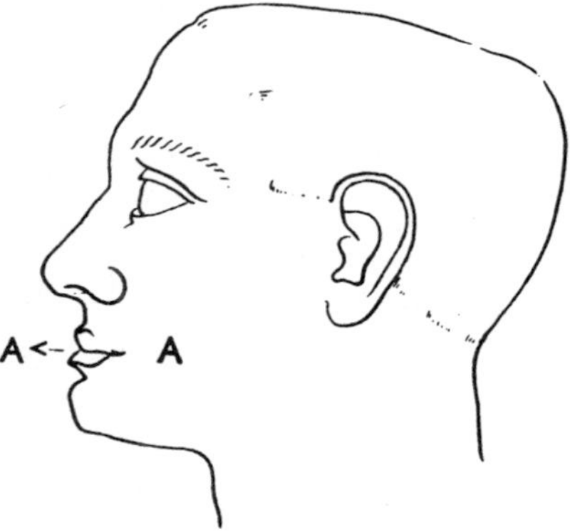

FIGURE 5. HORIZONTAL DIRECTION OF AIR MOVEMENT

feeling of pressure. The realization of this fact, together of course with the power of practical control, is the sure and never-failing remedy for the harsh and unmusical notes so frequently made by sopranos and tenors in their higher registers. A definite breath pressure must of necessity result in a horizontal direction of air movement as at *A A*, Figure 5, which means that a large proportion of the air is forced out of the mouth without being set into tonal vibration. Further, the same directional movement applied to the air in the sinuses would tend to drive the air forward against the walls of the sinus where exit is impossible, rather than the circling downward air movement which is required.

The vocal cord tutor impresses on his pupil the urgency and

necessity of thinking of beautiful tone, and trusts that with luck the vocal machinery will produce the exact sound quality which filled his mind. Listening to good tone for twenty years would never teach a student these facts of anatomy and mechanics. Were this possible we should certainly have had hundreds of Carusos, possibly thousands of Margaret Sheridans. The Sinus tone tutor teaches his pupil every detail of his vocal machinery, pointing out the various muscular parts which act automatically without any attempt at special control, so that the mind may be entirely concentrated on that part which needs, and answers to, will power. Then master and pupil are certain of getting good tone for the simple reason that they have brought into action mechanical principles and acoustic laws which we know will produce good tone.

The organ builder with a full knowledge of mechanical formulas works to produce an instrument which shall be beautiful in its solo effects and also in its full power. The Sinus tutor works on similar principles with the human material which is placed in his care. The master builder would never take an apprentice and tell him to listen to the beautiful tones of an organ and continue to listen until he could produce similar tones with a given amount of metal and wood. Every vocalist, yes and every speaker, whether it be parson, lawyer or member of Parliament, should understand every detail of his voice, and its absolute control, just as fully as he is supposed to understand the grammar of the language he speaks. Such an ideal need not be considered Utopian. When Sinus theories are generally accepted, and taught as orthodox principles ; then the training of voices will be carried out with much less trouble both to master and student than is the case at present. I have never yet found anyone who could explain to me why Welsh people usually have such excellent voices. One reason which has foolishly been offered is, ' Because of the music of their rippling rivulets.' There is no doubt that the Scotsman and the Devonian could properly claim rivulets and rivers which are not less musical than those in Wales, so such an attempt at reasoning, if it can be called reasoning, must be regarded as a failure. The explanation is to be found in the fact that the Cambrian in daily conversation invariably uses the upward inflection at the end of each sentence, thus keeping the frontal sinus in continuous use. It is astonishing how few people outside Wales ever use the frontal sinus as a matter of habit, and in my experience people are usually indignant at any attempt made to bring the frontal sinus into action. 'I like these low notes in my voice,' is the constant plea when an attempt is made to re-set the voice and make it more musical and more useful. To this protest one can only reply that the tutor cannot be responsible for the special likes or dislikes of the pupil who is being taught; all that the master can do is to direct the mind and the energy of the pupil into the proper channel which will lead to development. In this particular matter however one can always assure the pupil that bringing into action the frontal sinus[1] will never cause the loss of any low note, but is certain to develop the voice in every part of its compass, as well as in beauty and strength. This is not merely the statement of an interested person; it should be obvious to everyone that the *whole* of a machine can do better work than merely a part of it. The vocal cord theory of voice cannot possibly ensure bringing into use every sinus together with the full activity of the whole vocal machine. Sinus Tone Production is the only system for voice which gives to every part of the vocal machine its exact work to perform and explains the reasons for the structural conditions of both osseous and muscular anatomy. In the design of a motor car, in the arrangements for a new hospital, in building an organ, every tiny detail of size and shape has the most accurate attention, so that perfect working may be ensured with the minimum of energy. Such attention to scientific accuracy and design has never been possible with vocal cord knowledge, but it is now entirely possible on the basis of Sinus Tone Production.

[1] By the practice of the so-called falsetto voice.

CHAPTER III

THE CURATIVE FUNCTIONS OF SINUS TONE PRODUCTION

He that cometh to seek after knowledge with a mind to scorn and censure, shall be sure to find matter for his humour, but none for his instruction.—BACON.

THERE probably are very few statements in connection with vocal ideas which will not be contradicted by someone, but it is fairly safe to assert that previous to the publication of *Science and Singing* no definite and particular function had ever been assigned to the maxillary sinus, the frontal sinus, the anterior and posterior ethmoid cells, or the sphenoid sinus.[1] That being the case, it is obvious that no thought or consideration had ever been given to devise a system whereby their activity or usefulness could be either developed or controlled. Naturally under such unsatisfactory conditions their utility for the individual must gradually lessen and in some cases come dangerously near to the point of extinction. Now it requires no argument to prove that activity is an essential to healthy and useful life. If a squint in eyesight is not remedied by bringing the two eyes into parallel action, the imperfect eye gradually becomes blind through inactivity. A person who has experienced a broken limb knows only too well the atrophied condition of muscle which quickly ensues whilst a bone is getting re-set.

A reference to Figure 18 in *Science and Singing* will show that it is only the air in the sphenoid sinus which has a direct line of communication with the outside air. The ethmoid cells with their respective entrances are found behind the turbinated bones, and therefore the air in them is, as a general rule, less easily brought into action. The frontal sinus is probably the most difficult to operate because the air contained in it has to make a downward and backward movement along the infundibulum.[2] Consequently, it is an almost universal tendency to permit the

[1] See Appendix VIII.
[2] See Figure 2, page 30.

frontal sinuses to fall into disuse, and to confine the voice-producing air movements chiefly to the sphenoid sinuses.

The failure to cause an air movement in the frontal sinuses is the root cause of more disease than is likely to spring from any other single source. For many years we have known the serious dangers which result from phlebitis, constipation and embolism ; every medical practitioner would be horrified at any patients wishing to live for years in a room without any means of ventilation, but not a solitary person in the medical world has perceived the seriousness of having stale impure air in sixteen, eighteen or twenty cavities. It is known that a continuous circulation of the blood must be maintained, and that the food which we take into our bodies must be kept in motion ; the movement of air in the lungs has been talked and written of *ad nauseam* ; but the importance of air movement in the sinuses has never been visualized,[1] nor, until the science of Sinus Tone Production appeared, has any means been known of effecting it.

The absence of air movement, however, is only part of the trouble. Although medical men are aware of the fact, it may be well to remind other readers, that all these cavities, as well as the whole tract of the nose, are lined with a membrane whose function it is to produce mucus, which shall keep warm and moist the whole area to which it is attached. Pupils have said to me, ' I wish I could entirely get rid of this mucus,' to which I have replied, ' In that case you would be exceedingly ill, and would probably require medical attention for a long time.' The mucus serves useful beneficial purposes, in keeping the bone in good condition as well as acting as a purifier of the air before it enters the lungs. The wax in our ears serves a useful purpose, and so does the food we take into our body, but if these are allowed to accumulate, trouble quickly ensues. So it is with mucus. Its purpose is a

[1] My pupil the Reverend Sylvester Fryer, O.S.B., of Ampleforth Abbey, York, had a friend who was troubled with serious antrum infection. Knowing the benefit my pupil had received from the practice of Sinus principles, he questioned the medical specialist who had charge of his case as to his views upon the subject. The latter had no hesitation in scouting the idea of any air movement in the head cavities, stating, 'The air in the sinuses is always in a state of stagnation. How great would have been his horror at the thought of the air in the lungs being ' always in a state of stagnation,' or the blood in the veins in such a condition, but ' stagnation ' for the air in the cranial cavities he views with undisturbed equanimity !

useful one, but it must be kept moving or disastrous consequences will follow. The physician Galen in the second century wrote, 'Nature has made no organ for clearing away phlegm,' and that statement has been accepted until the present day. The hypothecation has stood because no one has seen any possibility of proving its incorrectness, but the marvel is that no one has seen the immense evil which must result from such a condition of stagnation. The practice of Sinus Tone Production not only keeps the head supplied with fresh air but prevents the accumulation of mucus in the cavities, and the congestion which brings misery and damaged health to millions.

It would weary the reader to give even a tithe of the beneficial results upon health produced by the practice of the Sinus method, but I shall venture to give three illustrations.

A lad of about twelve or thirteen years of age was brought to me. The flow of catarrh from his nose and mouth was practically continuous. For four months he had been treated at a hospital, without getting any relief. The condition of the lad was most pitiable. Lack-lustre eyes, sallow complexion, and a wearied tone of voice denoted absence of all energy. It was indeed a very serious case. We started work together and I showed him at the first lesson how to create air movements in the head. When he came the next week for his second lesson he was already feeling better, for the work I gave him just about doubled his output of mucus, and so we began to clear his head. At the end of three months his catarrh was only that which might be expected from a healthy individual, and the parents suggested he should discontinue his lessons. To this I was unable to agree, for I was certain that the mucous membrane in his head was still a long way from being in a satisfactory condition because the results of air circulation (that is the vocal tone) were not those which would come from free and unimpeded passages. I therefore offered to continue the lessons without any further fee, being convinced that the parents were unable to continue payment. At the end of fifteen months, I had the great satisfaction of seeing the lad with a keen boyish eye, a fine sharp tone of voice, and his cheeks an excellent colour.[1]

A case of a different kind, but equally serious in its way, was that of a school teacher in the employment of the Kent County Council.

[1] See *Musical Opinion*, June 1934.

She was about forty years of age. For several years her deafness had been increasing. Various aural specialists had failed to give her any relief and at length she was assured that hers was a hopeless case, in which the deafness would gradually increase, until at last she would be unable to hear anything. The forecast proved to be only too true and the poor soul became worse every year, and at length she visualized the possibility of having to give up her work. *And what then?* For two or three years she had refused to act on the advice of friends, who suggested she should try a course of Sinus work. To her mind the suggestion was ridiculous, but at length, being in desperate straits, she came to see me. I told her that most probably with patient work on her part, her trouble would gradually disappear. The work would be perfectly simple and could not under any circumstances do any harm, but it seemed to me it was well worth the trial. She agreed, and we made a start. After about four months she came to me with joy on her face and exclaimed, 'Mr. White, I can hear a watch tick!' Her general health naturally improved, she kept free from colds, and is now one of my most enthusiastic and grateful pupils.

My third illustration is the case of a lady who was over sixty-five years of age, and was suffering with singing noises in the head, for which the best specialists had been unable to provide a remedy. At our first interview I saw the case would probably be a very difficult one, and so it proved. My diagnosis was that mucus had become fixed and hardened in the sinus passages and hence the slight air movements which took place would give her the sensation of sound. Now I knew by experience that I could get her to produce an air circulation which would move fluid or semi-fluid mucus, but at that time I was uncertain if these air movements could shift a hardened mucus. Fortunately my client had the patience necessary for a full test and we were rewarded to our great joy with success, for the deafness was reduced to a condition which was really negligible and the head noises disappeared. Considering the very difficult circumstances of this case and the definite certainty with which experts had pronounced it to be 'incurable,' I feel that there is much cause for satisfaction and even joy at the therapeutic results of our twelve months' work.[1]

Repeated experiences such as these permit me to speak with

[1] See Appendix IX.

certainty of the terrible and very sad results which proceed from foul air and decaying mucus in the sinuses and their surroundings. Such results show themselves sometimes early in life, sometimes in middle age; sometimes the person arrives at sixty-five or seventy years of age before the penalty is demanded by nature, but sooner or later the penalty will be exacted. In my Sinus Tone Production booklet, published in February 1932, mention is made of quinsy, septic tonsils, pharyngitis, aphonia and the common cold as being some of the results, but this list is very incomplete. For some years past I have been aware and have proved that the practical application of Sinus theories will cure catarrhal deafness, pyorrhea, bronchitis, asthma, colitis, growths on vocal cords, and even the much dreaded phthisis in its early form. It is however a matter of great interest and importance that from independent medical authorities, and not from me, comes a further formidable list of human miseries which may spring from the same fount of infection. Thus, Dr. Watson-Williams in his book on *Chronic Nasal Sinusitis*[1] informs us that infected sinuses may cause lumbago, arthritis, eczema, appendicitis, eye affections and insanity. At first sight it would appear to be most unlikely that such an amazing and varied list of evils should spring from a single source, but Dr. Watson-Williams points out that the streptococcal or other germ will pierce the mucous membrane and then the bone, and may enter the blood stream, when of course its possibilities are almost unlimited. Should the germ pierce upwards, it may attack the brain, should it penetrate downwards it may attack the eye. Should it move along the air passages, the throat, bronchi and lungs are affected. Another authority[2] traces certain kinds of insanity to sinus infection. Finally, according to Dr. Thomas A. Poole, a nose and throat specialist of Washington, U.S.A., drug addiction begins in many cases with the congestion of the sinuses for the relief of which drugs are used. The resulting craving, he adds, can be cured if the primary pain is removed. He further states that a congested frontal sinus is liable to produce even criminal tendencies, which disappear upon the removal of the congestion.[3]

So far as I am aware, none of my clients has had criminal

[1] Published by John Wright & Sons, Ltd., Bristol.
[2] Dr. T. C. Graves of Birmingham. See *Lancet* for 16th June, 1934.
[3] See Appendix X.

tendencies, nor has any of them been addicted to drugs, so I am unable to express any personal opinion on these cases. But the vital point is that the medical authorities, whether they prove to be right or wrong in tracing any particular malady to sinus infection, can offer no effective means of dealing with that primary trouble. Dr. Watson-Williams gives most interesting explanations as to methods of detecting sinus infection, and many details concerning their cleansing from pus and their disinfection, but throughout the pages of his book not one word is mentioned relating to the *prevention* of pus and infected mucus. The attempt to drain the sinuses by surgical means is invariably only a temporary palliative and a painful one at that. Naturally the whole process of the sinuses refilling starts again after the operation and the poor patient has to resign himself to a helpless condition, realizing that either a creeping deafness is gradually overpowering him, or a frequently recurring bronchial asthma is reducing his vitality, or a never ceasing catarrhal condition is undermining his health with its attendant headaches, possible eye-affection, and other unpredictable consequences. But whatever diseases may correctly be ascribed to congestion of the sinuses, those diseases, however varied they may prove, can be combated, and if taken in time, cured, by the practice of Sinus Tone Production.

Some years ago I ventured to suggest to a pupil that the work of Sinus Tone Production would prove more valuable to humanity than Lord Lister's discovery of antiseptic surgery and the many blessings which follow it. My pupil was indignant at what he felt was my conceit and replied that my claim was ridiculous for it was not every one who lost his voice. To this I agreed, but ventured to remind him that it was not every one who wanted his leg or arm amputated. But it is possibly only a small percentage of the human family who pass through life without an operation of some sort or kind, and even the most trivial and insignificant cut on a finger must inspire gratitude to that very wonderful gentleman, Lord Lister, for discovering the principle of antiseptic treatment in dealing with open wounds. The great importance of Sinus theories is that by these means the surgeon's knife is avoided and disease and bad health are prevented.

For many years tutors have been insisting on the urgency of deep breathing, but it seems to me that the results, if not absolutely barren, are at all events poor and unsatisfactory. Dr. M. S. Pembrey[1] has said, ' The child does not require to be taught how to breathe, and with all respect to the Board of Education, there is no advantage in making children do deep breathing exercises.' A similar attitude towards the observance of deep breathing is maintained by Dr. Garnet Passe,[2] who states that ' as a means of attaining health, deep breathing may or may not be a desirable form of exercise.' Not a very helpful expression, but one which should make us pause and consider whether any advantages really can result from this over-emphasized maxim. Let this revision of thought sink deep in the mind of the reader, for although there is no imperative need to belittle the practice of deep breathing as it may do a certain amount of good, yet it is of small importance compared with the control of air movement in the cranial sinuses. So far as the lungs are concerned, deep exhalation is far more important than deep inhalation. If we give our personal attention to getting as much vitiated air as possible out of our lungs, nature will see to it that fresh air takes its place. It is an impossibility to *empty* the lungs, a pint and a half of air being about the minimum which can be left. Nature abhors a vacuum, and no more air can be taken from the lungs or admitted to them than the movement of the ribs will permit. When the ribs are fully raised and a deep breath is taken, this action permits from three to six pints of fresh air to enter the lungs, the air entering automatically as the ribs rise. When the weight of the ribs is released, then that gentle pressure sends air from the lungs. Hence to write as do some authors that the lungs must be filled at the base because they are broader there than at the top is nonsense. One cannot either empty or fill certain *parts* of the lungs in preference to other parts. To write as Blanche Marchesi does in her book, *The Singer's Catechism*,[3] of pumping air into the lungs is ridiculous. It is possible to pump air into a container if you require more than atmospheric pressure, but your pump needs a valve of some kind. In any case, air naturally fills every crevice of our ears, our skull and our lungs which is not otherwise filled.

What matters most, however, is the fact that our breathing system consists of a longer tract than the distance from the base

[1] Lecturer in Physiology at Guy's Hospital Medical School.
[2] *The Singing Voice*. Published by Sir Isaac Pitman & Sons, Ltd.
[3] Published by J. M. Dent & Sons, Ltd.

of the lungs up to the nose. When this is generally realized, then an important step will have been taken in making a huge improvement in the health of every individual. There is no special need to belittle the utility of the lung exercises providing always they are practised with proper care and skill. It is however a matter of the utmost importance to know that the nose does not constitute the terminus of the air system in our bodies, for it extends to the whole series of air cells or sinuses in the skull. If the air in all these cavities is frequently renewed, and so kept pure and fresh, the process will prevent the accumulation of mucus, and as a consequence there will be very little likelihood of lung trouble, or of any disease of catarrhal origin. The forty years of concentration which I have devoted to the possibilities of Sinus Tone Production, have shown results both vocal and therapeutic astonishing to those who have experienced them.

We will now consider the application of Sinus principles to stammering. Dr. George Cathcart in his pamphlet on stammering writes, ' Many theories have been propounded to explain the causation of stammering, but no two authorities agree.' This being so, it is not surprising to find that many and various are the ' remedies ' which have been suggested for the cure of this distressing affliction, but never have I come across any suggestion which could even pretend to be scientific. In no case, that is, has a definite principle been evolved for the cure. One gentleman, a Doctor of Music, assured me that a man of whom he had heard was absolutely cured, by drinking a pot of beer! A well-known medical man quite seriously asserts that eating barley sugar will assist in the cure, whilst a clergyman of my acquaintance was positive that a certain remedy was to be found in patting the left hand with the right as each word was said! Of course the bogy of bad breathing, no matter whether it is costal, clavicular, or diaphragmatic, is sure to be looked upon as a matter for correction. The importance of speaking slowly is usually and quite correctly emphasized. Mr. H. St. John Rumsey in his book, *No Need to stammer*,[1] remarks, ' Concentrate the mind on the vocal tone, which must be firm, smooth and even. The words should flow out in an even and continuous stream, instead of popping out of the mouth like corks out of champagne bottles.' The statement is undoubtedly true, and no one is less anxious to emulate in his

[1] Published by Methuen & Co., Ltd.

speech a champagne cork than is the afflicted stammerer. The same author gives admirable advice when, on the next page of his book, he writes, ' Speak smoothly and firmly and listen to the sound of the voice all the time.' The crux of the trouble is that voice will not come and the endeavour to ' speak smoothly ' ends in a disastrous and pitiable failure. There has probably never been a stammerer who was unaware that ' vocal tone should flow out evenly and smoothly.' What he wants to know is, what it is which prevents his vocal tone flowing out evenly and smoothly.

In a pamphlet entitled *The Modern Treatment of Stammering*,[1] the author writes, ' Stammering is a much greater problem than is usually realized and the provision of treatment is no light matter.' He then proceeds to suggest that deafness and errors in vision through causing uncertainty may produce stammering, and even ' the dreams of a stammerer may be of very great importance.' All of which goes to show that the worthy doctor is pursuing a false scent. ' Self-confidence,' he adds, ' is a long way to a cure.' Self-confidence, I am equally certain, will not advance the patient an inch towards a cure. The remedy is more scientific and much more exact than a mere feeling of self-confidence. Further, how can the individual feel self-confident when he knows full well by bitter and continuous experience that at any moment he may fall a victim to the vocal blight? Just as sensible and useful would it be to tell a drowning man not to allow himself to go under the water because so long as he has confidence the water would support him !

Mr. Herbert-Caesari suggests as a remedy, speaking ' on the principle of an aspirate, as an aspirate prevents rigidity in the throat.' The suggestion is interesting if only to give another example of the confusion of ideas which exists on the subject, for Mr. H. St. John Rumsey[2] asserts that the stammerer must ' increase the vocal cord resistance.' It seems to me that neither recommendation will go far in preventing a stammer, in fact in some cases Mr. Herbert-Caesari's advice would only intensify the difficulty. I had a clergyman stammerer, and he said to me, ' Mr. White, I dread coming to the fourth Commandment,' and his reason was the frequency of the letters *s* and *sh* ; with these sounds the air rushed forward out of his mouth and he could get

[1] By E. J. Bloome, M.B., Ch.B., D.P.A. Reprinted from the Proceedings of the International Conference on Speech Training, November 1927.

[2] Instructor for Speech Defects at Guy's Hospital, London.

no further with the word. Such unreliable suggestions as 'speaking on the principle of an aspirate' are better left unsaid, for the sufferer, finding how useless they are, sinks into further despair of ever finding a cure.

Equally futile is it to consider whether the person is right or left handed. People from whom we might have expected more intelligence have recommended this line of thought again and again. At the twenty-third annual Conference of Educational Associations held in January 1935 at University College, London, 'the left-handed theory of stammering causation' was explained during the discussion on remedial speech work by the chairman[1] of the section. He remarked that 'the two sides of the brain govern respectively the opposite sides of the body,' and elaborated on this theory. The report issued calls this 'a simple explanation,' but I should think it very doubtful if important practical results would issue from its consideration. In any case, it leaves the right-handed stammerer completely in the cold and without hope of remedy. At the same conference, Dr. Bloome stated that 'stammering, as is well known, is a nervous disorder.' Doubtless this theory is generally accepted, since a better one has not hitherto been known, but its therapeutic value is not apparent.

It should however be obvious that in all cases of stammering there are both physical and psychological factors to be taken into account. On the latter we shall have some observations to make; but inasmuch as Sinus work deals with the technique of voice production, it presents precisely the *physical* 'means whereby' stammering may be overcome. The physical explanation of stammering lies in the simple fact that voice is air movement, whilst speech is air movement plus muscular movement. When these two factors fail to work smoothly and in harmony a conflict is set up, the muscular movement opposing the air movement, or an improper air movement acting as a barrier to vocal tone. Thus the person stammers.[2] Here is the secret of the whole matter and here is the all-important starting point. I term it a secret only because this simple fact has never before been stated. Previously

[1] Dr. Millais Culpin, M.D., F.R.C.S.

[2] Mr. Rumsey, quoting *The Gateway of Speech* by Miss Freda Parsons, says, 'Speech is a muscle habit.' Had he said *consonants* are a muscle habit, he would have been quite correct, but speech is a combination of air movement *from the sinuses*, and muscular movements by the lips and tongue.

the word 'secret' has never been used in the literature of Sinus theories, their object being to clear up secrets and 'make the rough places plain.' With that end in view we will start in the systematic manner characteristic of Sinus principles.

The first lessons for the stammerer will not differ in principle from those of the singing pupil. When he has understood sufficiently the idea of Sinus Tone Production, he will be shown how to direct a tiny air movement downwards from the sinuses and so produce a vocal tone. All that I have written in the previous chapter concerning the importance of avoiding any muscular effort or movement applies even more urgently in the case of a stammering pupil. Air movement, and that only, is required to create the tone. Better speech results will be obtained if the flow of air comes from the frontal sinuses, which means that the tone produced will have rather a high pitch. The quality of tone required is what is misleadingly called 'falsetto.' The vowel *oo* (as in *fool*) will probably be the easiest sound on which to begin. When the pupil can readily induce a free flow of air, and therefore of sound, on *oo*, let him change the vowel to *e* (as in *red*), and then to *ah*. If the minimum amount of mouth movement is made in altering the vowels, the changes will come quite easily. The tyro invariably makes twice the amount of mouth movement which is needed and in doing so damages the tone he is producing. The changes from *oo* to *e* and from *e* to *ah* must be effected with a mouth movement so small that it can hardly be seen, and also without even the smallest muscular tension on the soft palate or pharynx. When this apparently simple matter can be controlled with ease, the consonant sounds must be studied.

A consonant is a sound caused by making some kind of resistance in the mouth to the flow of escaping air. This resistance may be formed by the lips, the tongue, and the teeth. Since stammering is caused by the interruption of the free flow of air, and by the attempt to overcome this interruption in the wrong way, by increased pressure, it will be apparent that the consonants offer particular difficulties to the stammerer (as they do, in a lesser degree, to the singer). What he has to learn to do, in articulation, is to interrupt or resist the tonal air-movement just long enough and just sufficiently to produce the wanted consonants, but not long enough nor violently enough to block the air altogether.

The first group of consonants to be considered consists of those formed by completely stopping and then releasing the air movement. They may be thought of as the ' full-stop ' consonants, and are those sometimes described as ' explosives,' namely, *b* and *p*, *d* and *t*, *g* (as in *go*) and *k*, *j* and *ch* (as in *church*). In the word *be*, the initial sound is made by first closing the lips and thus preventing any air movement, and then opening them, at the same instant starting the air movement from the sinuses, which movement must be continued for the vowel sound. A stammer is caused, as I have said, when the physical movements of articulation fail to work harmoniously with the air movements of tone production. In the case under consideration it is caused by a too heavy pressure of the lips on each other which prevents the air movement. The stammerer, not realizing this, continues pressing the lips together, until the effort becomes exhausted ; then the lips part and the *e* sound starts, because the air is allowed to move. Here we have the explanation. The next matter is the remedy. Let the pupil, very slowly and with the most gentle movement, allow the two lips just to touch each other, and then come apart, as in Figures 6 and 7. The tendency of the pupil will be to make a movement which is too big, as in Figure 8. This must be corrected. The very small movement as in Figures 6 and 7 must be made gently and with the utmost deliberation four or five times, without creating any sound. Then explain that the same movement is to take place without any added pressure, and the *be* sound is to come as the lips part. This having been successfully accomplished, add a final consonant and let the pupil say *bet*, the tutor watching with the greatest attention that no added movement or force is used. After this alter the vowel to *a*, so that *bat* is said, and again alter *bat* to *bit* or *bite*. Then let the pupil take such a phrase as, ' Big Bob bowled bad balls,' the eye of the tutor watching with the utmost keenness, that the learner does not take any extra breath, and that the minimum amount of movement and energy are used. Providing the tutor is sufficiently alert on these points, the stammerer will be delighted and astonished to see how simple is the remedy for stammering. A great deal more, however, remains to be learned, and brought under control, the latter being the chief difficulty. The pupil having realized the remedy for *b* will no doubt at once see that the same is available for *p*. We now take *t* and *d*, with very similar treatment. In this case we have to consider tongue instead of lip

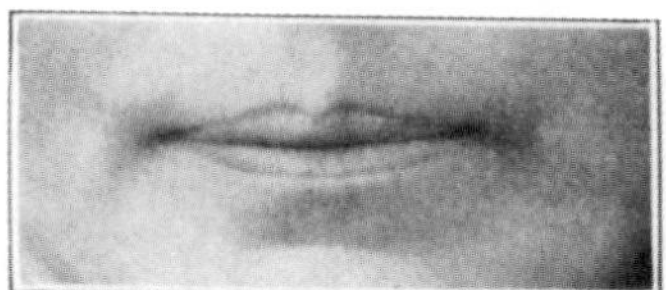

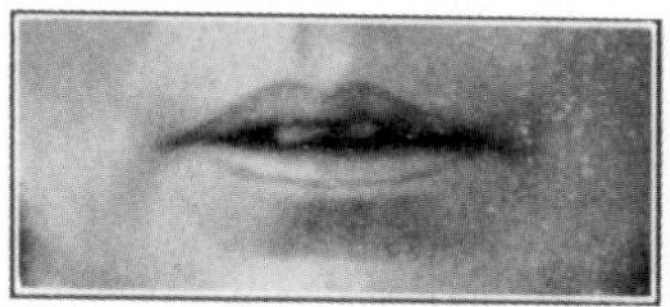

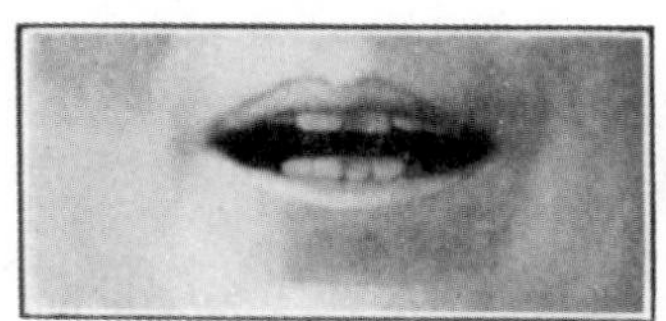

FIGURES 6, 7, AND 8. STAMMERING AND THE LIPS

movement. The course, however, is identical. Let the pupil very gently lift the tongue so that the tip touches the roof of the mouth just by the front teeth, and instantly falls down after the touch. The tongue must not remain at the roof for a single second, nor may any muscular energy pull it down ; the tip merely touches the hard palate and the tongue falls by its own weight. Let this action take place several times without creating any kind of sound. After this let the pupil with the same action add the *te* sound as the tongue falls, and afterwards alter the vowel as with the *b* exercise to *tar*, *tay* and *to* ; then if the tutor has done his work properly, the delighted student will be able after some days (or perhaps some weeks) of careful practice to say with ease : ' 'Twas the Telah Tabernacle Treat. Tiny teachers, tending tiny toddlers, thronged the Turnip Town terminus. Thoughtful Thomas took the tickets. The train tore through the tunnel to Tiptree.' After this practice with the consonant *t* little or no difficulty should be experienced with *d*. The principle of forming the sounds being understood, the remaining ' full - stop ' consonants should give little trouble. They are formed in the same way as *t* and *d*, except for variations in the point of contact between the tongue and the palate. It is most unlikely that the student who has grasped the idea for the *t* and *d* remedy will find any difficulty with the others. Should he do so, it is for the teacher patiently and helpfully to arrange some simple form of exercise or give the explanation which will put the matter right, but one can hardly conceive a pupil getting success with *b*, *p*, *d*, *t*, and failing with *k*, *g*, *ch*, and *j*. In the case of *g* and *k* special care may have to be taken to prevent any tightening or pushing the tongue upwards against the roof of the mouth. Should the pressure still persist, use the same kind of exercise and gentle movement of the tongue as for *d* and *t*.

We now go to the breath consonants, including the so-called ' sibilants,' which require different treatment and consideration. Each of these sounds, *s* and *z*, *f* and *v*, *sh* and *zh*,[1] and *h*, when it commences a word, has but one difficulty for the stammerer, namely, that he unconsciously directs the air out of his mouth for too long a time, with the result that an air movement in the sinuses is not created and that therefore sound or *voice* is an impossibility. Let the pupil fully realize that so long as the breath comes directly

[1] *i.e.*, the sound represented by the *s* in *leisure*, which is the voiced equivalent of the unvoiced *sh*.

out of the mouth, voice cannot be produced.[1] Now considering the word *see*, we have to understand that to form the consonant, breath *must* be directed out of the mouth, through a partial obstruction caused by the teeth. But this must be made as short as possible and be followed promptly by a transfer of activity to the sinuses to make the vowel *ee*. Clearly the same line of thought is applicable to syllables beginning with the other breath consonants.[2] The pupil must be shown that each of these consonants is made by breath escaping out of the mouth, and that this particular breath movement should be as short as possible. For practice, let the pupil say, or preferably sing, *ah* or any vowel sound, on some note which he or she finds easy. Let that note be held for as long a time as is convenient. Repeat the same three or four times, then prefix *f*, so that *far* is sung or said, and the student will see that there need be no difficulty in those two sounds. Go through the same course with each of the breath consonants, varying the vowels so that the pupil observes that the subject is now a system which can be controlled no matter what the vowel or the consonant.

It is very unlikely that any stammerer will need to consider and study all the sounds as explained here. The tutor must ascertain which sounds give trouble to the pupil and deal with those only. When the elementary principles of speech have been thoroughly grasped, it will in some cases be advisable to get the student to say quite smoothly a few short sentences, such as 'Nor can I come'; 'Give me a pen'; taking care that the phrase consists of words of one syllable only. It is also very advisable that words starting with breath consonants should be avoided at the outset, because their use necessitates a break in the down flow of the air from the sinuses. When the exercises already suggested are under some kind of control, then use any words to

[1] See *Science and Singing*, page 18.

[2] Nó reference has been made in the text to the distinction between 'voiced' and 'unvoiced' consonants, because hitherto it has not proved to be of any practical importance. I have never, that is to say, met a stammerer who, having learnt how to say *p* or *f*, still experienced any difficulty with *b* or *v*. But cases may possibly arise in which a realization of the difference would prove helpful to teacher or pupil. An unvoiced consonant, such as *t*, *s*, or *f*, is caused solely by obstructing the outgoing breath in the mouth.. The corresponding voiced sounds, such as *d*, *z* and *v*, are the result of combining such obstruction with the air movement from the sinuses.

form a sentence, being careful that the frontal sinus position is maintained. This is a most important matter and the stammerer's cure depends upon it. It is advisable at this stage to avoid words of three or more syllables.

So far as the separate sounds are concerned, this covers the difficulties of a stammerer in starting words, and no stammerer ever finds a difficulty in finishing them.

The next point for consideration is the speed at which the pupil attempts to speak. With very few exceptions an endeavour is made to get as many words spoken in one breath as possible, and that most probably without any realization of too quick an utterance. When the pupil is shown the speed at which conversation should be conducted he invariably considers it to be unnaturally slow, and so it is to him, because in his vigorous endeavours to make speech, he has become accustomed to get on as quickly as possible when once a phrase has been started. He therefore has to train himself to a steady and, so far as possible, an even pace.

In bad cases, the afflicted person may make facial contortions. I had a lad about eighteen years of age, who opened his mouth in a ridiculous manner, lifting his eyebrows as well. Of course nothing could be done until these antics were either stopped or eased. When it was explained to him that these movements were the result of an overflow of electric energy from the brain, it was like pouring oil on a stormy sea, although the soothing results took longer for accomplishment. Yet one could detect at once the lessening of both pressure and movement. This was the cause of the greater satisfaction because the treatment he had previously received from orthodox and recognized specialists had aggravated rather than relieved his trouble.

There are three other details for which the tutor must be on the alert in order to rescue his client from this misery of uncontrolled speech. We say advisedly the tutor must be on the alert, because he must himself watch the pupil without appearing to do so, in order to discover if these matters, with which we are about to deal, enter into the stammering condition. Should the pupil fortunately be free from them, then on no account should any mention of them be made. In any case the pupil has quite sufficient difficulty in speech control, without bringing to his knowledge any troubles of which he may possibly be unconscious, but might contract if brought to his notice.

It will have been observed by all who treat stammering cases that it is quite a usual occurrence for the person to read fairly fluently, but if he is unexpectedly asked a question, a block at once takes place when a reply is attempted. The sufferer has not the faintest notion what is the cause of this apparent paradox, nor has the tutor usually any remedy to suggest. The explanation is as follows. The stammerer being suddenly confronted with a question, instantly, although unconsciously, makes a physical and energetic effort to make an immediate reply. Putting the same fact in another way, he turns on (of course unconsciously) so much electric energy, that the whole current overflows its intended channel and is expended on the person's physical self, and no air movement can take place. A useful analogy may be seen in the working of a motor car. A man I know purchased a car and came in it to see me. After our interview he re-entered the car, but could not get it to move. Having spent five or six minutes in vain endeavours to make it start, he at length realized that the throttle was fully open. He closed it down, and the car was soon off, every part functioning properly. Let the stammerer realize that this is exactly like his speech difficulties. We will not however leave him to work out his own vocal salvation by means of similes, however good they may be, but will give the exact directions which must be followed. (*a*) No attempt should be made to give an immediate reply to a question. Three or four seconds should elapse before any sound is attempted. This slight pause may seem a long one to the person who makes it, but in reality it is nothing but a tiny wait, so that he may have the opportunity of visualizing or mentally rehearsing those *means whereby* he can produce an even flow of speech. During that slight wait any undue rush of energy or power will have had the opportunity to die down. With the cessation of pressure, the student, carefully bearing in mind the necessity for *downward* air movement, will make a gentle attempt to form the first word of the sentence. When this plan is explained for the first time to the pupil, he usually retorts, 'That is all very well, but I want to get on with my reply, and cannot wait to go through all that mental consideration.' The proper reply to this argument is, 'Unquestionably time and patience in a bountiful measure are required before a cure can be attained, but there is certainly no more time spent in awaiting the subsiding of the energy cyclone, than is spent in the useless and vain endeavour to act whilst it is surging.' Speech cannot possibly proceed whilst this muscular energy is over-active, and if the pupil will wait until it has subsided, then with the use of the downward air movement, speech will easily flow without having drawn the attention of anyone to the struggle for speech mastery. Further, there is the great satisfaction of knowing that every time the double control (that is muscular control and air control) is mastered the patient is a step nearer to automatic speech. (*b*) Some people when excited feel a disturbance around the solar plexus which interferes with speech. Fortunately this condition does not operate with every stammerer, and the tutor must ascertain in an unobtrusive manner, if his client experiences the difficulty. A direct question on the point should on no account be put, as this might possibly involve a beginning of the trouble which had not previously existed. Should the trouble exist there is only one remedy, and that is to wait until the energy has subsided. The pupil is usually very loth to observe this wait, for every second appears to be a whole minute to the would-be speaker, yet undoubtedly it is the only way by which real control of the vocal machine can be attained. Speech cannot be produced whilst this particular kind of turmoil is at work at the solar plexus, and a battle between the two forms of energy will always mean a win for the muscular force. First concentrate on subduing the turmoil and the unwanted and misplaced energy will in time cease to make itself felt, and speech will no longer have this difficulty with which to contend. (*c*) Yet another point to consider here is one of great difficulty for both master and pupil, because it is impossible to form exact laws which will overcome the trouble. Our ideas so far have dealt with mechanical facts, now we must deal with the psychological. It is not unusual for a stammerer to begin to reply to a question with some preparatory sound. It may be *Er* or *Mm*. One client I had always started with *And*. If he were asked, 'What is the time?' he would reply, 'And I think it is half-past four.' If one queried, 'Do you think you could do this?' 'And I am afraid not,' would come the answer, with a long-drawn-out *And*. The idea at the back of his mind was that *And* made a start, and with the start once made he might with a little luck get out the reply. Needless to say, such a habit must be stopped, in a very kind and sympathetic manner, but quite definitely.

The next matter is more difficult to eradicate. A question having been asked, the stammerer will in his customary manner make a dash at the reply, before the sentence is quite complete in his mind. The result is that there will be hesitation and blocking in the middle of the sentence, not because of an obstruction in word formation, but because he started speaking a sentence before his mind had conceived the full answer, or it may be because in the middle of the sentence it dawned upon him that there was a better way of finishing it, and so the two phrases, either of which might have completed the sentence, get jammed. The remedy, as with other speech difficulties, is to 'hasten slowly.' Do not start a reply until the whole phrase has been visualized, then begin at a deliberate pace.

In most cases, speech education should commence with an explanation to the pupil that there are four kinds of sounds, namely, the vowels, the full-stop consonants, the breath consonants, and the 'half-stops,' sometimes known as 'liquids.' The mechanics of the vowels require first attention, then the full-stop consonants which usually are the most fruitful source of trouble, and thirdly the breath consonants. If the control of these be understood, it is unlikely that the liquids *m* and *n*, and *l* and *r*, will give any trouble. Lastly the psychological aspect must be considered. There is no need to make this order a constant rule ; it is suggested as being one which will in most cases be of assistance to both tutor and pupil. It is, however, important that consideration of mechanical laws for speech should precede the psychological, and for the following reason. Directly the pupil can see that a principle for speech is possible, there is invariably an added interest to the study. He can then be thoroughly assured that by perseveringly following the principles enunciated, he may be certain of a successful issue. He is shown that there is no need for a blockage on a word beginning with *d* or *t*, as he only has to be careful not to press his tongue against the roof of his mouth. I say 'only,' but the tutor and pupil will have to realize that this cessation of pressure will need considerable practice and care, because the pressure habit has been formed and carried on sometimes for years. With children who have had stammering parents the tendency is established from the beginning. This, however, need not bring about a single thought of failure. The cure is certain with perseverance in the right principles.

That the principles are correct can be demonstrated with exactitude and precision to the pupil, but practical success must not be expected at once merely because the pupil understands the method; he has to learn its definite control. The first step is the inhibition of what to him is the natural tendency, and the second step is the gradual personal control of the laws which govern speech. 'Interference with the functioning of an organism always means reduced efficiency,' and stammering is nothing but an interference, unconscious though it be, with the even movement of the vocal machine. Sinus Tone Production being a science gives a co-ordination of movement and conduct, and speech is dominated by intelligence and brain power instead of by instinct. 'False valuations lie at the root of much mental disease,' remarks a well-known lecturer, and it is the false valuation of the vocal cords, and the resulting chaos which springs from it, which has the responsibility for all stammering. Stammering exists only because people believe that voice proceeds from the throat level, and consciously or unconsciously place their speech activities too low. Mr. H. St. John Rumsey has said in an article on stammering, 'Nine-tenths of the cure rests with the stammerer himself.' If this be correct, it would seem to be of little use going to a specialist for cure. Mr. Rumsey states the remedy will be found in stressing the vowels. Possibly there may be some truth in the suggestion, but as we have already pointed out, one of the major difficulties consists in words commencing with *d*, *t* and *b*, where the block occurs before the vowel is reached. In such cases it is useless for the tutor to tell the pupil to 'stress the vowels,' for the simple reason that he is unable to get to the vowels. When he has reached the vowels the difficulty is past for that particular word.

In *Guy's Hospital Gazette* for 26th September 1937 Mr. Rumsey makes an attack on my work. He certainly does not mention me by name but as at present I am the only lecturer on Sinus Tone Production and was asked to lecture at the school to which he refers, there can be no doubt as to whom he alludes. The subject being of great importance, I propose to deal with it fully although sympathetically. My critic correctly says that 'the audience listened with close attention' to me at the school and adds 'No one present asked how, if the sinuses acted like organ pipes[1]

[1] I did not give this simile.

a singer could sometimes sing out of tune or readjust to the accompaniment of a piano of slightly different pitch.'

It is true the question was not asked, but had it been asked it would have been easy to reply that it was just as possible, and, *if you knew how*, just as easy, to tune and control voice as to tune an organ pipe. He then continues : 'Until elocution is on sounder lines with some guaranteed knowledge of voice production and the mechanism of speech, it is obvious that much harm may be done by asking an elocutionist to correct a stammer. This harm would indeed be almost certain, inasmuch as speech training by elocutionists is generally limited to the teaching of overstressed consonants.'

Whether it is correct to say that 'speech training by elocutionists is generally limited to the teaching of overstressed consonants' I will not debate, but probably the tutors at the school would have a different opinion. When the students at Guy's Hospital are told that in studying Sinus Tone Production the harm done 'would indeed be almost certain' because of overstressed consonants, then it will be perfectly evident to my readers that he has not even an elementary idea about Sinus theories. The person who is willing to learn has been shown on pages 70-1 how to *avoid* stressing consonants in order that the vowel sound may easily follow. Mr. Rumsey writes, 'A full explanation of stammering is no easier to give than a full explanation of electricity.' No doubt this is correct whilst we adhere to vocal cord theories, but the Sinus tutor, although confronted with serious difficulties in dealing with his client, has very definite lines on which to move and act. In the issue of the same journal for 11th September 1937, another article on the same subject appears from the same pen and at times is tantalizingly near the truth. For example : 'The stammerer by increasing consonant resistance at the expense of the flow of vocal tone upsets the correct balance between the two so that for the moment speech becomes impossible.' So far this is excellent, but when an attempt is made to suggest a remedy we get no further than the expression of a result which the person wishes to effect without getting any hint as to how—that is to say the *means whereby*—it is to be accomplished. We are told, 'The remedy is obvious, the stammerer must concentrate on the outward flow of tone rather than on the movements which convert that tone into words ; so it is necessary to form a mental picture of a smooth flow of vocal tone passing through and out of the mouth. . . . Thus the mental picture of a firm vocal tone solves the problem of inco-ordination.' With all due respect to the Instructor for Speech Defects at Guy's Hospital, it would be just as sensible to say that the mental picture of a mansion in Park Lane solves all the difficulties of poverty. To make a mental picture 'of a smooth flow of vocal tone' is a perfectly simple matter, but it will not help in the very least to produce it, and especially is that the case if the person thinks of the flow of tone coming out of the mouth.

The following experience I had with a pupil will give an interesting and very useful example of error and remedy in speech.

The gentleman with whom I was dealing was about forty-three years of age, and had been a lifelong stammerer, notwithstanding many attempts at cure by those who professed to provide a remedy. After several lessons my pupil was able to carry on a conversation quite easily, but was less successful when reading or in making a speech. At one lesson in reading, the word *entitled* occurred. He said *en*, but blocked at *t*. Having overcome this difficulty he assured me that the reason he was unable to get the complete word was that he had not sufficient breath. To which I replied, 'My dear sir, on the contrary, the reason of the block was that you had too much breath, so much in fact, that with the tongue pressed against the upper teeth, the *i* sound was unable to start.' He was not convinced, so I proved my point in the following manner. I asked him to take a full breath, then slowly to let it out. When he had exhaled to nearly the full extent, I said, 'Now say "entitled,"' and instantly out slipped the word without the smallest difficulty, thus proving to the astonishment of my client that it was the superabundance, and therefore the pressure, of breath that in the first place prevented the easy enunciation of the word. This particular instance is given only to show the natural but incorrect and fatal habit of stammerers of inhaling about three times the amount of air required for ordinary speech, a habit which is intensified by the foolish ignorance of those tutors who direct their pupils to practise exercises in deep breathing. The correct tuition should consist in showing the stammerer how to control the air which is already in the sinuses, and not to overcharge the lungs with air and so produce the very pressure which should be avoided. Similarly words with an initial *s* sound, although not making an absolute block, prevent the vowel sound being reached. The tutor on the lines of Sinus Tone Production can with precision remedy every detail in the defect, by showing his client how to reorganize his speech machinery, so that it may run with smoothness and perfection.

In the pamphlet already mentioned on page 67 Dr. Bloome gives a very illuminating example of a stammer cure, as follows: 'Two British officers who stammered went to India and there had to learn Hindustani; they lost their stammer. Was it because of the sing-song speech, or was it because they lost their inferiority complex in dealing with the natives? The fact remains that they were cured.' It has been said that common sense is a divine gift, but it seems to me that only a very elementary sense of perception is needed to see that the cure was effected by 'the sing-song speech.'

In this kind of speech the tongue and lip movements for consonant production are reduced to the required minimum, whilst an even flow of air, creating vowel sounds, is maintained through the sinuses. Having been compelled to adopt the so-called 'sing-song' speech for producing Hindustani, these men quite naturally adopted a similar course for their native tongue. It is well known that the troubles of a stammerer disappear when he sings. Let him then observe that the speaking and the singing voice should be *one* thing and not two separate and distinct things as he makes them. In *Science and Singing* I have explained that 'any person who can speak is capable of song also,' a statement which in this volume I would reverse, and say for the comfort and encouragement of the stammerer that anyone who can sing can speak also, and of course I mean speak fluently and with perfect ease. As I said in the paragraph just quoted, there is no change whatever in the mechanism used or in the parts affected. Differences arise because the stammerer, without intending to do so, makes a pressure for consonants in speaking which he does not make in singing. Further, his mind being concentrated in singing on the melodic flow of the music, he minimizes the difficulty of the consonants and gives more value to the vowels. With the added fact that no psychological difficulties arise it will, I think, be seen that a satisfying explanation is here given why a stammerer can sing, but not talk. The explanation, too, will fill the mind of the student with a definite certainty that he *can* be cured, and this is an important matter. Only too frequently the sufferer is forced to the conclusion that his case is hopeless because all remedial measures have failed, and perhaps because he has heard the opinion that 'for the adult stammerer the only hope of cure lies in auto-suggestion.'[1] When therefore a new light with fresh possibilities dawns on his reasoned intelligence, the psychological effect is of great use, for the abject fear which has hitherto dominated his mind, producing a condition of conflict, gradually clears away. A clear, logical and controllable system comes into his power, and the conflict gradually becomes a thing of the past.

In passing from song to speech, a course similar to the following is frequently of great help to the pupil. Play quite slowly a simple passage such as

and direct the pupil to sing *Ah* to it. Then alter to

No difficulty is likely to occur in doing this. Now ask the pupil to sing

The student with the aid of the singing tone is almost certain to get through these phrases without difficulty. Now let the same words be repeated in a speaking manner on a similar pitch to the reciting note F. If the tutor has done his work properly the phrases will be said without a flaw. It is almost needless to say that any words may be taken for the purpose. 'Drink to me only with thine eyes, and I will pledge with mine' will do, or a couple of lines from Shakespeare, the point being to make a connection in the mind of the pupil between singing which is found to be easy, and free speech which is believed to be impossible. A further word of warning to the tutor is the fact that the musical pitch I have suggested may not be suitable for every voice. That is a matter which must be settled by the judgment of the master.

[1] *Stammering*, by Elsie Fogerty. Published by Allen & Unwin, Ltd.

Should he select a tone which is unsuitable for the purpose, he must not expect success. Experience plays a large part in making the selection. In this, as in every detail concerning voice, the tutor must be expected to take infinite pains in dealing with the problems as they arise, for no good work can ever be accomplished without experiencing difficulty. 'If a part directly employed in an activity is being used in a comparatively new way which is still unfamiliar, the stimulus to use this part in the new way is weak in comparison with the stimulus to use the other parts of the organism which are being indirectly employed in the activity, in the old habitual way.'[1] The student must not be disappointed therefore to find the old habit of producing pressure, forcing itself on him again and again, but by degrees this reaction will weaken and after many an annoying struggle will die and disappear. The cure of stammering, no less than the development of the singing voice, illustrates the importance of 'the principle of ceasing to work in blind pursuit of an "end" and of attending instead to the *means whereby* this "end" can be attained . . . . for by no other method can he get the better of his old sub-conscious habits, and build up consciously the new and improved condition which he is anxious to bring about.'[2]

Although, so far as I am aware, this was not written with any special reference to stammering, yet it indicates the exact *modus operandi* that the learner must observe in the endeavour to control voice on the lines of Sinus Tone Production. We will suppose as an example that a father says to his stammering son, 'James, would you like to go to Margate with me to-morrow ?' The lad instantly visualizes the joy of getting to Margate and with that end in his mind wishes to say, 'Please, father, I should.' But not having a correct co-ordination of speech mechanics, he gets blocked at the consonant *P*, the lips being firmly fixed together so that he cannot reach the vowel *e*. The energy which fixed the lips in due time becomes exhausted, and then, and not till then, the lips part, and the lad manages to say, 'Please, father, I,' by which time his breath requires renewing, so he takes a big breath and proceeds to waste it all on *sh* by sending the breath in a forward direction out of the mouth. The energy of the second attempt

[1] *The Use of the Self*, by F. Matthias Alexander. Published by Methuen & Co., Ltd.

[2] *Constructive Conscious Control of the Individual*, by F. Matthias Alexander. Published by Methuen & Co., Ltd.

having evaporated, the poor lad eventually gets the *ou* sound because there is no further supply of air to force out of the mouth. In order to avoid all this struggle and state of warfare, let the lad understand the *means whereby*; that he must not take any extra breath, nor may he use any more energy than if he were sitting still in a chair quietly reading a book. This subject might be lengthened to a considerable extent, but probably sufficient has been explained to make fairly clear the path which the stammerer should take to arrive in the delightful land of the 'Voice Beautiful.'

CHAPTER IV

THE CHALLENGE OF SINUS TONE PRODUCTION

Child of Nature, learn to unlearn.
BENJAMIN DISRAELI, EARL OF BEACONSFIELD.

IN *Sir Alfred Fripp's Life Story*, it is related that on a certain occasion early in his career, he happened to be at Marlborough House, having recently become on calling terms with Prince Eddy. In passing through one of the passages be met Oscar Clayton, who was physician to the Prince of Wales. Dr. Clayton, instead of generously extending to the young man a welcome, showed evident annoyance and blurted out, 'Young man, what are you doing here ?' In the light of history it must unfortunately be admitted that a large number of medical men would have acted in a similar manner. '*Young man, what are you doing here* ?' fairly indicates the attitude adopted by the medical profession generally towards every one outside its own particular circle and to a great many within it who dare to suggest any trace of originality in medical matters or anything better than the accepted way.

The notorious cases of Dr. William Harvey (1578–1657), Sir James Simpson (1811–1870), Lord Lister (1827–1912), and Sir Ronald Ross (1857–1932), make a very incomplete list, which at the present day is being continued. In the magazine issued by University College Hospital in December 1930 there is a review of Dr. Percy Hall's book on *Asthma*. He suggests a new treatment based upon ultra-violet radiations, and the critic says, 'Dr. Hall does not appear to expect to be believed, but we sympathize with him.' It would seem an almost unbelievable state of affairs that the medical profession receives £139,000 per annum for research work,[1] and yet when men in their own profession put before their eyes facts of the utmost value, which have been thoroughly tested during years of private research, the heads of the profession refuse to give these results either consideration or even a hearing.

The Conquest of Disease, by David Masters, deals in a pointed

[1] This was the sum provided in the Vote for Scientific Investigation in 1932. Presumably this may be taken as an average.

but not too severe manner with this subject of blind medical jealousy. Insulin, the only remedy for diabetes, was first given to the world in March 1922 by F. G. Banting, a young Canadian doctor, and David Masters remarks, 'Insulin is practically the first great discovery in medicine that has silenced all scepticism and been immediately accepted by the medical profession.' With other discoveries, 'medical history merely repeated its sorry self.' 'Insulin is the one new discovery which was hailed by the medical fraternity with paeans of praise, one discovery which silenced the jealous tongues of the doctors, and was accepted without question. It is little that the doctors can boast of in this respect, so let it be recorded in their favour that they practically accepted insulin without a cavil.' Possibly one reason was that Dr. Banting unfolded his plans to the authorities of Toronto University. Had he lived in Great Britain, would he have been treated with as much reason and respect? But very fortunately Toronto University 'had faith in him, faith which Banting has fully justified; but think of what the world would have missed if they had sent him away.' Surely it is a huge pity that such a noble calling as that of the medical profession, with gifted men toiling unselfishly in it, should have such a blot on its past and present that it can be truly said by a modern writer, that 'medical history has merely repeated its sorry self.' Thus medical records endorse Hegel's remark, 'We learn from history, that we do not learn from history.'

As this attitude constitutes the state of the medical mind now as it did 300 years ago, it can hardly be a matter for surprise that people outside the sacred medical colleges such as those courageous pioneers Thomas and Hutton, the first I believe of the manipulative surgeons or 'bone-setters,' with their successors, Sir Herbert Barker and the late Mr. Blake, should be treated without even decent respect. Thus, Sir Herbert Barker writes: 'For the art of manipulative surgery I have waged a protracted, exhausting and at times almost heart-breaking fight against the entrenched prejudice of a powerful, rightly State-protected, and close corporation. Not very long ago no abusive epithet or scorn was too virulent to apply to me or my work.'[1] To-day, however, a scholarly and highly esteemed chairman of the General Medical Council, Sir Henry Brackenbury, writes that 'the earlier neglect

[1] *Daily Telegraph*, 7th February 1935.

of the profession of the methods of manipulative surgery constitutes one of the most tragic omissions in medical history.'

The fact is too easily forgotten that a very large proportion of the progress made in science and art has been the work of original thinkers and workers without influence in the universities, and will probably continue to come from similar sources. Thus, '*Young man, what are you doing here?*' may be the welcome extended by the medical profession to this volume, as it has been (with a few exceptions, which I gladly admit) to my previous work. Yet I dare to prophesy that one day in the future—near or distant —the neglect of Sinus methods will be included as a 'tragic omission in medical history,' and by that time possibly even the Royal Schools of Music will deign to give the matter some consideration.

I recognize, however, that there is some reasonable excuse for the medical man's failure to see the force of all my arguments, as the science of acoustics necessarily has not entered into his studies. Ernest Newman remarks that 'various attempts have been made to find a rationale for the statement that "architecture is frozen music," but the endeavours have all broken down because the theorizing architects know too little about music and the theorizing musicians too little about architecture.' In a similar way we may correctly say that medical men with their ample knowledge of anatomy know hardly anything of acoustics, and physicists with their knowledge of acoustics know very little of human anatomy; while musical people with their knowledge of 'suspended discords,' 'false relations,' and musical history, to say nothing of the French, Italian and German languages, have but a very elementary knowledge of acoustics, and none at all of human anatomy, save the endeavour to talk in an airy manner about 'the shock of the glottis' or 'inflating the lungs.'

The claim of Sinus Tone Production to rank with the discoveries of Lister and Ross and the other pioneers is based upon facts readily ascertainable if they are not already well known. Consider first some of the ills which orthodox medicine is still unable to cure. 'If we can be taught,' the *Daily Telegraph* once declared, 'to live down the common cold, there will be no limit to our gratitude.' Every year four out of ten men and seven out of ten women are temporarily disabled by colds, and many a cold, being neglected, has developed into pneumonia and bronchitis with tragic results.

It is a perennial reproach to which the medical profession is subject, that in spite of advances in so many other fields, it has neither been able to prevent nor to cure the common cold. It has even been suggested that, because of its very commonness, and the benign, if annoying, course that it usually runs, the cold has not been treated by the profession with the attention that it deserves. That is certainly untrue. The trouble is that, although the cold is so familiar a visitation, its exact cause is considerably more obscure than that of many severer and more dangerous complaints.[1]

In January 1928 Mr. Francis Garvin, President of the Chemical Foundation in America, made a gift of £40,000 to the Johns Hopkins University and Hospital at Baltimore, so that a five-year study should be made of the causes and consequences of the common cold. That five years' course was completed a long time ago, and so far as I am aware, no practical results have come for the benefit of mankind. America is not slow to make known her discoveries—in that respect she is far wiser than Britain—and the discovery of any reliable and scientific means of cold prevention would soon have been communicated to Europe. Nearer home, two trustees of the late Sir Henry Royce are administering a fund established with a large part of Sir Henry's estate of £110,000 for research into the causes of and cures for the common cold. Sir Henry died in 1933, and it is quite clear that the paid research workers had made no discovery up to November 1936, for the issue of *The Times* for November 21st of that year contained a leader giving an account of tests made by the Chief Medical Officer of the Post Office as to the value of inoculation against colds. 'Volunteers were invited from various typical large towns and some hundreds were inoculated in the autumn of the three years 1933 to 1935. There was a large "control" group. It was found that over the whole group and for the whole period there was practically no reduction of sickness among the inoculated as compared with the uninoculated. Nor was improvement observed among the inoculated after inoculation; in other words, colds and other catarrhal troubles were neither prevented by inoculation nor limited in their spread.'

England for nearly thirty years has had the remedy at her

[1] This statement is taken from an anonymous newspaper article, 'By a Doctor.'

disposal, without the expenditure of thousands of pounds, but those who pose as medical authorities turn a deaf ear to the fact that Sinus theories have proved the possibility of clearing the head from those germs which are the source of colds.

> Alas ! the gratitude of men
> Hath oftener left me mourning,

wrote William Wordsworth, and even the promised voice of gratitude from the *Daily Telegraph* has not yet reached my ears !

Another trouble which refuses to yield to orthodox remedies is deafness. A responsible surgeon[1] has expressed his regret that in spite of fifty years' study and experience they had not progressed far in its treatment. 'I do not think,' he said, 'we can yet hold out any hope of giving hearing back, and we should warn the patient that, in spite of our treatment, we may fail to stay the progress.' That was the experience of a client of mine, and Sinus principles provided a remedy which the medical profession does not possess. In cases of disease where operations are necessary then the surgeon's skill is a matter for admiration and for the patient's gratitude, but there are many cases where surgery is useless.

It will not be disputed that there is still a great deal of unnecessary suffering involving a considerable sacrifice of life.[2] 'We have been accustomed for generations,' it has been said, 'to repeat glibly that prevention is better than cure, but we have done little to apply that doctrine in matters of sickness.' Let our medical men remember, like Coriolanus, that 'there is a world elsewhere,' namely a world of tremendous possibilities for good and bad health, in the head cavities. When these are brought under the control which we exercise over other parts of our body, then preventive science will have doubled its powers.

When *Science and Singing* (the first book ever written on the art of Sinus Tone Production) was published in 1909, one reviewer said, 'We very much doubt if the average vocalist even knows that he possesses a sinus.' The criticism was correct, but since that date both the medical and the musical professions, finding the important part the sinuses play both for vocalism and health,

[1] J. B. Layton, Surgeon to the Throat and Ear Department, Guy's Hospital. (Royal Sanitary Institute Health Congress, Bournemouth, July 1935.)

[2] See the memorandum on preventive medicine issued by the Chief Medical Adviser to the Ministry of Health in 1926.

have been devoting more and more attention to the study of them, with immense advantage to tutor, pupil and patient. It is then a matter of some importance to know that at a meeting of the British Medical Association held in September 1923, Mr. V. E. Negus, F.R.C.S., a throat specialist, gave a lecture which was reported in the following terms:

> There was an array of the larynxes of all kinds of animals, reptiles and birds in the room where Mr. V. E. Negus, who had carried out experiments in Sir Arthur Keith's laboratory, made revelations in regard to the new function of the vocal cords. Mr. Negus explained that his investigations were not very definite, but it seemed that the vocal cords had not a great relation to the voice. He illustrated his point by saying that the cow could make quite a variety of sounds and yet had no cords at all. His theory was that the larynx was developed by the animals which used their forearms for pulling and the same applied to human beings.

It is evident that the investigations of Mr. Negus were 'not very definite.' One might quote Charlotte Brontë and say they were 'shadowy, like half-comprehended notions that float dim through children's brains.' Yet we have here an ominous breaking with orthodox ideas, and the same surgeon further emphasized his departure from ancient custom in his book *The Mechanism of the Larynx*.[1] In this, a chapter on the purposive use of sound was 'written with the intention of discovering to what extent, if any, a set plan is laid down by the organ of hearing or the higher centres of the brain, along which the evolution of the mechanism of sound production must proceed; I would suggest that any such directing force is slight.' From this it is evident that Mr. Negus has formed the opinion that a 'set plan' for the development of the 'mechanism of sound production' is not at present available. Moreover he admits that 'there are, no doubt, many fallacies in the reasoning put forward to ascribe a function to the vocal cords and to the ventricular bands, but it seems to me that in the main the observations may be correct in spite of obvious deficiencies.' This is indeed 'thinking in shadow,' and when a first-rate throat specialist can only write of the accepted ideas on vocal cords that they 'may be correct in spite of obvious deficiencies,' it must surely indicate that a welcome should await an explanation which bears closer examination.

Sir Milsom Rees in lecturing before the British Medical

[1] Published by Wm. Heinemann & Sons, Ltd.

Association at Belfast (1937) made the following interesting and important statements: 'When one bears in mind the very small percentage of the population who can sing in any sense that can be called singing, the much smaller percentage who can sing really well, the relatively few who take up singing professionally, the fewer still who make a success of it even after years of serious training and great expense, one is led to the conclusion that singing is not a natural endowment, that the vocal cords were not constructed by Nature for singing purposes. Singing is an acquired accomplishment, into the service of which have been pressed certain organs not intended for it. The same conclusion is suggested by the multitude of troubles that afflict even the best singers.'

To show that the vocal cords 'were not constructed by Nature for singing purposes' is the very object of this book. Our laryngologist, however, gives us only negative information, which although we regard it sympathetically can hardly be called helpful. Sinus theories provide not only an intelligible and constructive medium for voice, but explain how to act thereon. Probably Sir Milsom would oppose all belief in the creed of the Sinus tutor, but some further information he gives should make the most confirmed vocal cord theorist pause and consider if all is well within that ancient orthodox fold.

At the beginning of this lecture our authority asserts (and many will agree with him) that 'in singing the vibrations originate in an expiratory current from the lungs passing the edges of the vocal cords and setting them in motion, just as in the violin the pulling of the string creates the air waves and forms the note.' Here are two points for consideration: (*a*) Do we want our vocal cords pulled, and if we do, (*b*) can the air pull them?

One might blow on a violin string for ten minutes or more and not get sufficient tone to fill even a tiny room, much less Queen's Hall. The contention sometimes advanced that the vocal cords are alive in no way helps to uphold the comparison and as an argument has already been demolished. In reality there can be no real simile between the action of the air passing between the vocal cords and the pulling of the strings of a violin with a resined bow.

Another point in the lecture for notice is the reference made to 'the force with which the voice is projected' by the operatic singer. 'These high notes with heavy volume mean an enormous strain with subsequent exhaustion.' Small wonder then that 'Singers' voices inevitably deteriorate with age,' and even during the height of their career are liable to nodules on the cords, loss of elasticity of the fibres, catarrhal troubles, and laryngitis, as Sir Milsom Rees admits. Naturally this condition of things makes plenty of work for the throat specialist, in fact one is reminded of the burglar who said to the judge of assize, 'It's blokes like me what keeps blokes like you.'

Sinus principles will undoubtedly lessen the work of the throat specialist. A prophecy made by the lecturer will probably in due course be fulfilled. It was as follows: 'With more definite methods of teaching, greater experience, some anatomical knowledge, and care of the vocal cords, the best voices are yet to be heard.' We are not told what are the 'more definite methods of teaching,' but here are the means in Sinus theories, and those who have studied them know with what precision they work.

So the final considerations which I have to bring forward, in justification of the challenge of Sinus Tone Production, are concerned with the anatomy of the throat. Just as the 'different departments of mathematical physics are closely connected, so that the solution of a question in one branch of the subject admits of being transferred into another branch and serving as the solution of a corresponding problem there,'[1] so the recognition of the true source of voice in the head sinuses enables us to assign their true functions instead of imaginary ones to the vocal cords, the false vocal cords and the sacculus laryngis. An explanation has been offered in *Science and Singing* of the functions of these little understood throat organs, but we are now able to give fuller details than have hitherto been possible concerning them, and show that all the minutiae of anatomical detail bear the wonderful impress of design for their action.

Sir Milsom Rees in the lecture quoted above informed his audience that the false cords act as a damper on the outer part of the true cords in order to produce falsetto. He does not appear to have given any explanation of this extraordinary behaviour on the part of the false cords. The assertion would appear to make considerable demands on one's credulity for the following reasons; A falsetto tone of voice, although small and possibly—but not invariably—weak, is usually of a bright quality and quite different

[1] Sir Joseph Larmor.

from a tone which has been damped. Further, it is extremely difficult to see how the false cords are to descend from the position which they occupy in order to come in contact with the true cords with which they are not even in line. I trust that my explanation of falsetto voice[1] and the unfolding of the following beautiful details in design of the so called false cords will give a more satisfying and reasonable solution of their activities.

It has long been known to the medical profession and to a few people in the musical world, that the 'true' vocal cords point upwards and the 'false' vocal cords point downwards, but the present volume contains the first attempt to give any satisfactory reason for these conditions. The term 'vocal cords' should be altered to 'breath governors,' as that term does convey to the mind the work which the vocal cords really perform.[2] They are triangular in shape and point upwards so that they shall meet at a fine point and thus form the least possible resistance to the air column. Let the reader refer to Figure 9 and observe to what a beautifully fine point the air is brought at the top of the windpipe. In this figure the actual vocal cords cannot be seen, but their position at *A* is indicated, and it will be readily understood that two very tiny strips of membrane, triangular in shape and pointing upwards in the direction in which the air is moving, would so control and direct a column of air with the least possible resistance and with the utmost certainty and fineness. As sound *producers*, the cords would be in as bad a position as they could well be. If the creation of tone were the task of the vocal cords one might well expect them to be strung from the point *D* to a position on the opposite side of the windpipe about half an inch lower, thus giving a good length of tone-creating material. The length of string is the smallest possible in the windpipe with a consequent minimum of sound producing material. Compare these details with those of the ear (Figure 11), where the tympanic membrane, the sound *receiving* material, is placed not at right angles but at an angle of about 55 degrees with the lower and anterior walls of the external acoustic meatus, by which disposition a comparatively large surface of membrane is exposed to the vibrating air for the reception of sound waves. And so, as in all the Creator's works, we see function and design in agreement. Once again, as *voice*

[1] See pages 54 and 55, also *Science and Singing*, page 51.
[2] Appendix XI.

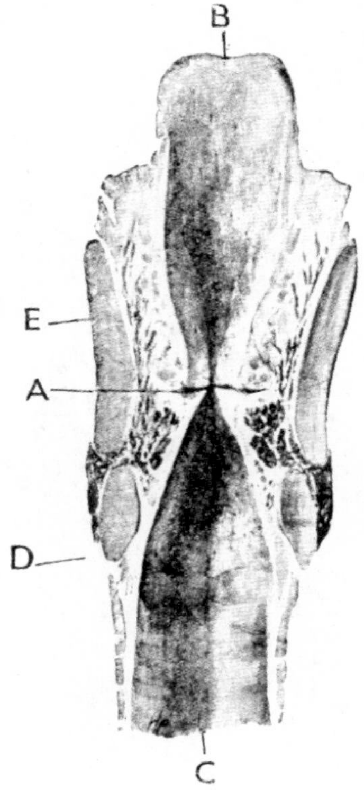

Figure 9. The Windpipe, with the True and False Vocal Cords, from behind

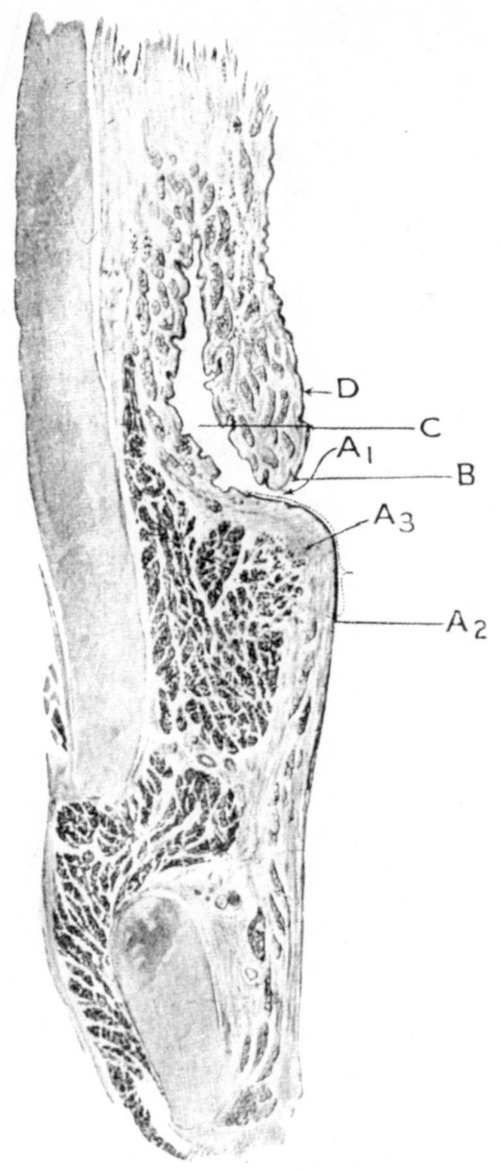

FIGURE 10. THE TRUE VOCAL CORDS, THE FALSE VOCAL CORDS, AND THE SACCULUS LARYNGIS (LARYNGEAL POUCH), MAGNIFIED FIVE TIMES

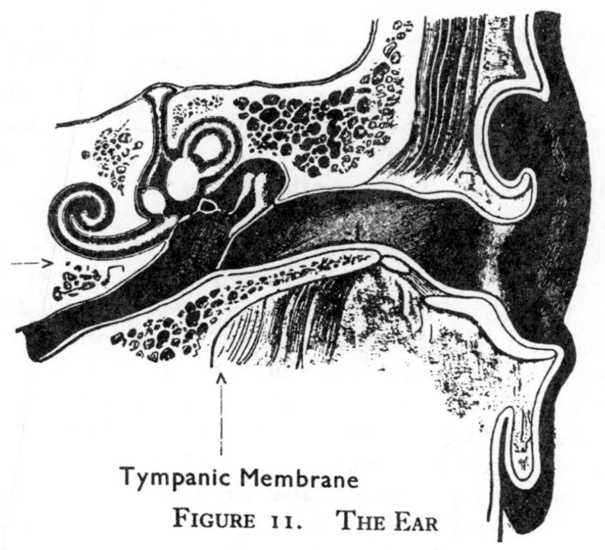

FIGURE 11. THE EAR

producers, the vocal cords in pointing upwards are arranged in a manner distinctly inimical to their work. Had they been set at right angles, or pointing downwards, the air would have been better able to produce vibration in them, but as *breath governors* their position could not be improved ; it is ideal.

Let us now consider Figure 10, where we have a veritable mine of information which has eluded our scientists and the workers in medical research. Let me, however, hasten to acknowledge my indebtedness to the medical profession for having discovered the anatomical facts, this being a work which I have neither the means nor the opportunity of pursuing. I would that the medical profession were as willing to acknowledge my work in assigning reason and utility to the facts. It must be noted that appreciation of the wonderful material and mechanical efficiency of the larynx as part of the vocal machine, depends in the first place on the acceptance of the idea that it is not here that vocal tone is produced. The figure shows the left side of the larynx, as though Figure 9 were cut in half from *B* to *C* ; and the length shown from *D* to *E*. In the first place then, note the dotted lines between *A*1 and *A*2. At *A*3 the vocal cords are situated and the dotted lines mark an area that is provided with a special type of epithelium or membrane, known medically as the stratified squamous type. The membrane above and below this area is ciliated, that is provided with hairs which by their vibratory action keep the mucus moving upwards, and it has glands from which the mucus flows. All this membrane adheres quite loosely to the surrounding tissue, but that which immediately surrounds the vocal cords adheres quite tightly to the subjacent tissue, and has neither glands nor hair.

Looking upon the vocal cords as *breath governors*, it is not difficult to discover a reason for this reversal of nature's order in this one spot. Certain it is, that it could not be a matter of mere chance. Because of the absence of looseness, cilia and glands from the membrane, the vocal cords are free to form, and direct into the head, a tiny and steady column of air. The cilia standing above the membrane, and the glands creating orifices below it, would tend to damage an even flow of air whilst a loose membrane would lessen a perfect control.

The next point to notice is that the false vocal cords at *B*, Figure 10, are set slightly back from the true cords at *A*3, thus ensuring a perfectly free air passage without any liability of their creating an involuntary obstruction. The sacculus laryngis at *C*, Figure 10, has been already described and explained in *Science and Singing*, but a further detail of much importance is made evident in Figure 10, in consequence of the magnification of this section of the larynx. Those readers who have well studied Figure 29 in *Science and Singing* are already aware of the work which the Sinus worker gives to the false vocal cords and the laryngeal pouch, but it will perhaps be well to repeat the details here.

The term 'false vocal cords' is a complete misnomer, for the cords have nothing whatever to do with voice. Their function is to *prevent* the passage of air into the mouth, nose or head, or in other words to make when required an air-tight compartment, with the diaphragm as the base, and the top of each closed chimney in the sacculus laryngis as the other end of the enclosure. So when we want to lift a heavy weight, we take a big breath and prevent that breath escaping by the apposition of the two false cords, and it will at once be seen that the greater the pressure we use, the more firmly are the two sides of the chimneys pressed towards each other. The cords and the membrane above them are supplied with muscular fibres, and so strength is given for the purpose. The true cords have no muscular fibres and could not possibly resist a strain, both because of their great elasticity and also because of their position in pointing upwards. And so we have the true vocal cords pointing upwards, in order to avoid all strain and resistance, while they control a moving column of air; but we have the false cords pointing downwards, in order to direct the air from a central position into the sacculus on each side, and so block the air movement as with a valve.

In *Quain's Anatomy*, (Vol. II, Part 2), the following passage occurs:

> Wylie showed (*Edinburgh Medical Journal*, 1866), that when the plicae ventriculares[1] are simply approximated, and air is injected into the larynx from below, they prevent the exit of the air, and he held that the closure of the glottis in defaecation and vomiting is mainly effected by their apposition. His experiments have been confirmed by Brunton and Cash.

A passing statement like this does little justice to the exquisite details of this tiny section of the throat. When pressure for defaecation is required, it is not 'mainly effected by their apposition,' but entirely effected in this way. Nature has given us no other means of getting air pressure. So we repeat the false cords point downwards, so that they may be able to direct the air into the saccule, which they would be unable to do if they pointed upwards or even towards each other.

The next detail is one which, so far as I am aware, has never been noticed in any text-book of anatomy. It will be noticed that the whole of the inner surface of the tube from *A2* downwards is quite smooth, but the whole of the membrane connected with the sacculus laryngis is rough and uneven. This texture ensures that the section at *D* shall not adhere to that which is on the opposite side, which it might easily do after air pressure in the sacculus. It will also prevent the two inner walls of the sacculus clinging to each other, and thus entire freedom of movement is attained. It would be impossible to conceive any structure, human or otherwise, where function and design are more exquisitely balanced, or better fitted to work harmoniously together, than is shown in all these details of the larynx when considered from the point of view of Sinus Tone Production.

'All great facts of concrete existence are demonstrated by what is called a cumulative proof, that is, one made of many arguments all leading to one point, each one strengthening the other and by

[1] *i.e.*, false vocal cords.

their union forming an overwhelming body of evidence.'[1] To the reader who has followed me so far it must be evident that the art of Sinus Tone Production has the great advantage of 'cumulative proof' to attest its truth. Let us glance over the facts. In the first place Sinus theories settle what musical instrument the human voice most nearly resembles. So far as I can judge that much-disputed honour belongs to the ocarina. In this little instrument there are no strings to suggest tension. There are no springs to suggest organ reeds, nor any material that needs renewing as in the case of the oboe. Although the instrument does not enter into the ensemble of the orchestra, yet I have heard a player produce tone of beauty and power from it. It is purely a wind instrument of the flute family, without having the length of a flute. As with the voice, a small volume of air under exact control is the chief necessity for the instrument.

In the second place, Sinus principles explain with definite precision anatomical details concerning the shape and position of the vocal cords, the false vocal cords, the uvula, the sinuses, the infundibulum and the diploe; all of which have hitherto been unexplained and mysterious in their functioning. They reveal a very wonderful harmony between design and function, which we have shown to be entirely absent in vocal cord theories. A control of diaphragm, ribs, larynx and soft palate is cut out of the student's syllabus, for the simple reason that in a natural condition the vocal machine is ready for use. It follows that the singer is relieved of the necessity of making additional muscular movements for vocalism.

The next point of evidence is the satisfaction experienced by many who had the desire to sing but apparently were denied the ability. Yet on attempting a control of the cranial cavities (of course under the direction of a competent tutor), they found to their joy that a good singing voice was quite within their capabilities, and this notwithstanding the oft-repeated opinion expressed by voice specialists, 'You have no ear.' Apparently the ear was at fault, for the pupil was quite unable to produce any note which was suggested, but these seemingly insurmountable difficulties entirely disappeared when Sinus principles were carefully set forth and practised.

[1] Canon Bagshawe, D.D., in *The Credentials of the Catholic Church*. Published by Burns, Oates & Washbourne, Ltd.

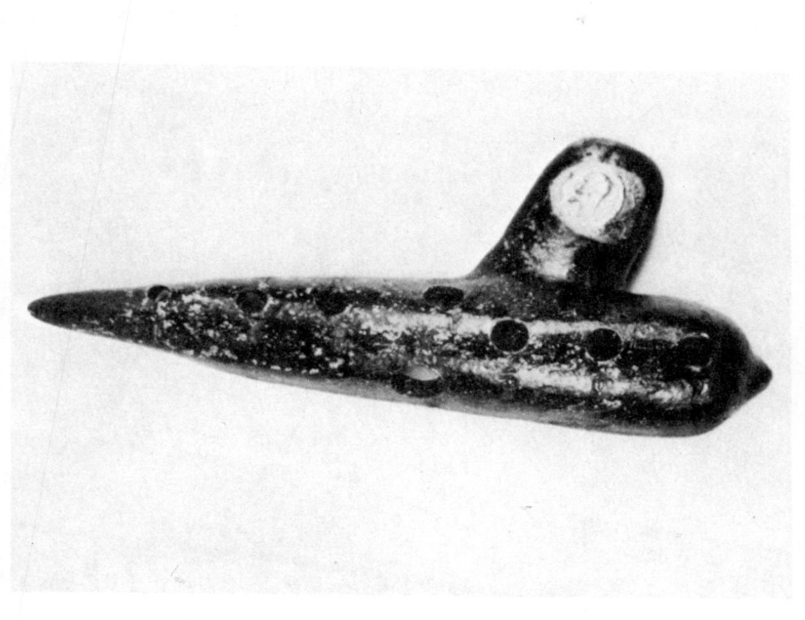

FIGURE 12. OCARINA

The next proof we will take from the speaking voice. Much has been written and a great deal more might be written on this aspect of the subject, but I think that the quickest and most satisfactory way at this moment is to make reference to *Light on the Voice Beautiful*, where nine people, including medical men and clergy, bear testimony to the cure of aphonia when all expectation of recovery had disappeared. *Light on the Voice Beautiful* was published in 1930, and many additional cases have since had attention with equally successful results, so that the Very Rev. Canon Pritchard, for example, can write, 'I have every reason to be noisily grateful to Sinus Tone Production.'[1]

We pass on then to the singing voice. Examples of singers who have owed their success to Sinus training have been given in a previous chapter; and while still no artist of widespread fame can be claimed as a product of this work, yet there are by now many hundreds, if not thousands,[2] of people who have had the opportunity of hearing and enjoying the results of Sinus practice. 'A man's virtue,' said Pascal, 'should not be gauged by his efforts, but by what he does usually.' So it is by the general level of excellence, or more emphatically still, by the universal *improvement* of its students, that Sinus Tone Production is endorsed.

The next step in the cumulative proof is the scientific test. We have seen on the authority of Sir Edward Bairstow, Howard Fry, Field-Hyde and many others, that vocal cord training is not scientific. Sinus Tone Production is scientific inasmuch as it 'begins with measurement,' assigns an exact physical cause for every vocal result, works in accordance with acoustic laws, and explains the 'means whereby' perfect tone may be produced. The last but certainly not the least cumulative proof is the curative power of Sinus practice. By this I refer to the relief which it has afforded to serious ill health such as asthma, deafness, catarrh, and all those diseases which are due to not keeping the head cavities in a clear, healthy condition.[3]

'The useful combinations are precisely the most beautiful.'[4] We have here a useful combination of seven separate and distinct

[1] See *Musical Opinion*, August 1933.

[2] Thanks to broadcasting, there is no danger of exaggeration here.

[3] See *Musical Opinion*, August 1933, June 1934, and January 1936; also *Musical Times*, August, November and December 1936; also *Catholic Herald*, 9th, 16th, 30th April 1937.

[4] Monsieur Poincaré, *Science and Method*.

proofs of Sinus Tone Production, not one of which can be paralleled by the vocal cord theory. As Sir Percy Nunn concluded, after personal experience of Sinus work, 'when a theory points to specific details of practice and the practice faithfully observed, leads to such gratifying results as I (and many others) bear witness to, there is at least a *prima facie* case for thinking that the essential features of the theory must be sound.'[1]

[1] See *Musical Opinion*, January 1936.

CHAPTER V

THE ARTIST

I worked with patience, which means almost power—ELIZABETH BARRETT BROWNING.

PROBABLY there is nothing I can add to the subject of artistry which has not been said before. Nevertheless I may be able to say a few words which may be useful to the earnest student, and it is with this hope that Chapter V is added.

It would perhaps be challenging to say that Sarah Bernhardt was the greatest artist who ever lived, but it would be safe to say that there have been few greater. The great artist W. Graham Robertson, writing of the 'divine Sarah,' said, 'She never spared trouble—in fact, I do not think she realized the meaning of the word. Nothing connected with her art was a trouble; she would always give her best.'[1] Let every aspirant to success, whether it be in the art or business world, remember and always act on this principle, and there will be fewer failures to chronicle and more beauty in the world. The late Bishop Gore was never tired of saying, 'There is no failure except in ceasing to try.'

An example of persevering courage and determination which is useful to every student, but especially to the novice who is working on Sinus theories, is the history of the Liverpool and Manchester Railway, designed and carried out by George Stephenson, who began his career as a child at twopence per day and afterwards earned sixpence when he started work at the colliery.[2] Not indeed a very exciting start for a young lad; and when, a few years later, he was, through sheer ability and pluck, fighting his way to the front rank in the engineering world, his contemporaries with recognized positions 'did not relish the idea of a man who had picked up his experience at Newcastle coal-pits, appearing in the

[1] *Time Was.*

[2] These and the following facts are taken from *The Life of George Stephenson*, by Samuel Smiles. Published by John Murray.

capacity of a leading engineer before Parliament, and attempting to establish a new system of internal communications in the country.' When parliamentary matters were eventually settled in favour of the Railway Bill, George Stephenson began on that part of the work which had been declared to be 'impossible,' namely, to make a road over Chat Moss upon which the railway could run. This, it had been stated, 'no man in his senses would undertake to do.' Michael Drayton supposed the Moss to have its origin at the Deluge, and certainly nothing more impassable could be imagined than that dreary waste of liquid mud on which nothing could stand or even rest.

The greatest difficulty was experienced in forming an embankment upon the edge of the bog at the Manchester end. Moss as dry as it could be cut was brought up in small wagons by men and boys, and emptied so as to form an embankment; but the bank had not been raised three or four feet in height, ere the stuff broke through the heathery surface of the bog and sank. More moss was brought up and emptied in with no better success, and for many weeks the filling was continued without any visible embankment having been made. It was the duty of the resident engineer to proceed to Liverpool every fortnight to obtain the wages of the workmen employed under him; and on these occasions he was required to colour up, on a section drawn to a working scale, suspended against the wall of the directors' room, the amount of excavations, embankments, and other work executed from time to time. But on many occasions, there was no progress whatever to show for the money expended on the Chat Moss embankment. Sometimes, indeed, the visible work done was less than it had appeared a fortnight or even a month before!

'There was no help for it,' said George Stephenson, 'but to go on. An immense outlay had been incurred, and great loss would have been occasioned, had the scheme then been abandoned, and the line taken by another route. So the directors were *compelled* to allow me to go on with my plans, of the ultimate success of which I myself never for one moment doubted.'

The Worsley and Trafford men who lived near the Moss and plumed themselves upon their practical knowledge of bog work, declared the completion of the road to be utterly impracticable 'If you knew as much about Chat Moss as we do,' they said, you would never have entered on so rash an undertaking; and depend upon it all you have done and are doing will prove abortive.' Such were the conclusions of science and experience. In the midst of all these alarms and prophecies of failure, George Stephenson never lost heart, but held to his purpose. His motto was 'Persevere.' 'You must go on filling in,' he said. 'The stuff emptied in, is doing its work out of sight, and if you will but have patience it will soon begin to show.' So the filling went on, and by 1st January 1830 it was completed, and formed one of the best parts of the road. A good example of unflinching perseverance in artistic work is found in Sir Charles Santley's book, *Student and Singer*. 'Towards the end of March [1865], I made my first appearance in Italian opera in my native town at the old Theatre Royal. It seemed like a dream to find myself on the stage which I had ten years before contemplated with longing eyes, without a ray of hope that I should ever appear on it.' Let this 'ray of hope' ever illumine the mind of the vocal student. 'Success in life is a matter not so much of talent or opportunity as of concentration and perseverance.' The Sinus student will frequently have need of Ben Jonson's simile, 'When I take the humour of a thing once I am like your tailor's needle—I go through.' It may be admitted that it is not a thrilling or exciting experience to practise daily, for weeks and months on end, a few simple exercises, not with the object of learning the exercises, for these could be learned easily in five or six minutes, but with the object of watching with the greatest care the tone and quality of voice which is being produced. You are then doing what George Stephenson called the 'filling in.' Here is the same work repeated with unvarying regularity, so that a voice of excellent quality may eventually appear.

'By perseverance the snail reached the ark,' said the Reverend C. H. Spurgeon, and the *bon mot* is an excellent one for the memory of the Sinus student, because his patience is subjected to a far greater strain than that of the vocal cord student, who is usually directed to learn volume after volume of vocalizes, such as those by Lablache, Bordogni, Nava and the inevitable Concone. Doubtless the learning and singing of these interesting melodies would be more entertaining than practising technical exercises, but it necessarily means that the attention of the student is divided between giving a correct rendering of the melody and watching the vocal machine. While the pupil is working at the technique of Sinus training, he is unable to spare any thought for the interpretative aspect of the music, as the whole mind must be concentrated on vocal control and that alone. Interpretation has separate study and is never neglected, nor indeed is any point in the vocal outfit overlooked.

The failure to give attention to apparently little things is the cause of many blunders. Graham Robertson says that he saw Bernhardt rehearse *La Dame aux Camélias*, and was interested to note 'the absolute precision with which she built up her apparently spontaneous effects.'

Madame Emma Calvé in her book *My Life* gives an interesting example of patient perseverance. She writes, 'I remember on one occasion she[1] made me repeat a phrase from the mad scene of Ophelia eighty separate times. I was ready to cry with nervousness and exhaustion when she finally allowed me to rest. 'That will do very nicely,' she remarked tranquilly, at the end of the ordeal. 'You are worthy of being my pupil, for you are beginning to learn patience.' Let it be noted however that patience is as necessary for the tutor as for the pupil. Each should ever have in mind the Dutch proverb, 'An ounce of patience is worth a pound of brains.'

Another artist of a different kind, namely, Sir Harry Lauder, writes,[2] 'I have to pay tremendous attention to detail, and I have always done so since first I went on to the stage. I've studied with enormous care the tiny things that folk like—it might be the very angle at which I shake my stick, or the exact half tone of a confidential joke . . . some gestures I've studied and practised to such a pitch that they look spontaneous—and there's nothing more difficult.'

Docti rationem artis intellegunt, indocti voluptatem,[3] wrote Quintilian. Thus it is the duty of the student to study every possible aspect of his work from every possible angle, so that every detail has had thorough consideration with meticulous care. Then will he have learned the full theory of his art, and the layman will be able to enjoy its pleasures. I will give you one or two

[1] Madame Laborde, who was then teaching Madame Emma Calvé in Paris.

[2] *Wee Drappies*. Published by Hutchinson & Co.

[3] The instructed understand the *means whereby* of art, the ignorant only its pleasure.

illustrations. One of my pupils offered his services as a tenor to a church at Kingston. The organist before accepting him tried his voice up and down the scale. Being unable to find a break or flaw in the voice, he turned to the applicant with the remark, 'Your voice seems to go up naturally.' Said my pupil to me afterwards, 'He little knew the amount of technique which I had to practise in order to get that "natural" result.' 'Art is only work utterly unspoilt, and drudgery is only art gone utterly wrong.'[1] The example of a lady may be interesting. This pupil started lessons with me, but at the end of a year was so disheartened with what appeared to be slow progress and continuous corrections that she thought of discontinuing the study. She determined, however, to try a little longer, and at length improvement began to be more obvious. Thus encouraged she worked with greater enthusiasm and is now a professional vocalist with a continually increasing list of engagements. The point of the story is yet to come. She entered as a competitor at one of the many musical festivals which are held all over the country, and was awarded the first prize, the adjudicator asking her to repeat the song, because he so much enjoyed her singing, and as an example to the other competitors. The said adjudicator was one of the most unbending and outright opponents of Sinus theories who have appeared in the press. Yet he unhesitatingly singled out the Sinus trained vocalist as being the best singer, without of course having the slightest knowledge as to the training she had received. Here we have the student instructed in the theory of her art (Sinus Tone Production), giving pleasure to the adjudicator, unlearned in that particular system. He does not to this day know the secret of this lady's success.

Continuing on the lines of our Latin quotation, we will consider another vocal matter which affects very considerably both the learned and the unlearned in our art. I refer to diction. It is the one point in vocalization which the unlearned can correctly criticize, and none but the vocal student can appreciate the difficulties of clear enunciation. The subject is dealt with in Chapter VII of *Science and Singing*, but it is hoped that the following suggestions may be useful to the student, if not to the tutor. I have permission from the composer and publisher to use Roger Quilter's song, *Fill a glass with golden wine*, as a model for

[1] C. E. Montague.

my suggestions. The first six bars are printed (of course quite correctly) as follows:

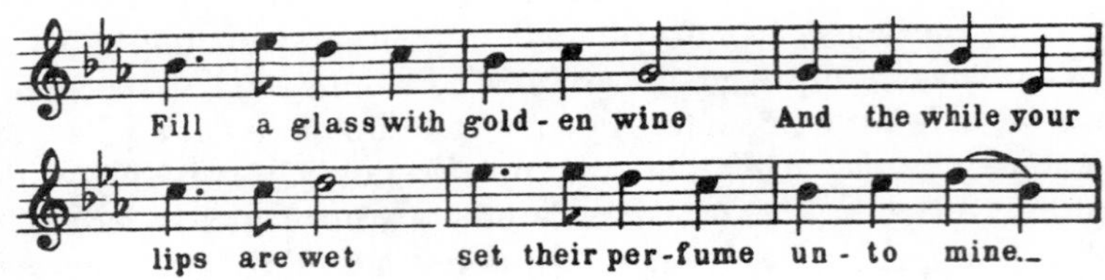

If the student will think of the words as printed below, it would enable him to get a big improvement in the tone of the song.

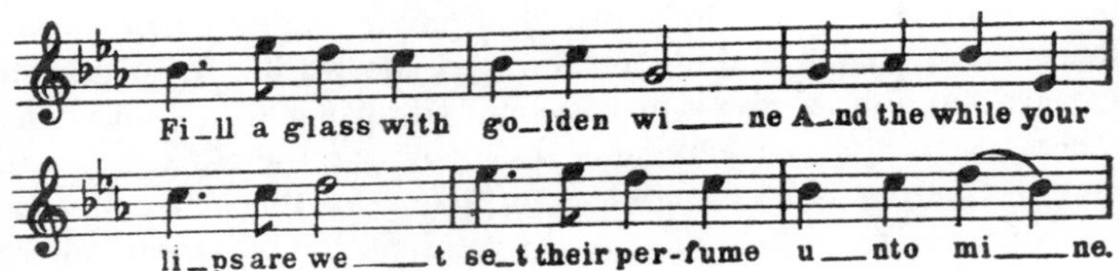

I have heard some of the best-known singers prolong the crotchet on the *ll* of *fill* instead of vocalizing as long as possible on the *i*. Similarly, on the words *lips* and *set*, instead of keeping to the vowel sound as long as possible, they have gone directly on to the consonants *p* and *t* with the result that the vocal tone has been shut off. On the minim D the tone should be prolonged on the *e*, leaving the *t* until the last possible second. The last two notes on the word *mine* are frequently sung as though the word *mine* was a two-syllable word *mi-een*, instead of taking the two notes on the vowel *i*. A word of warning. Let the student beware lest he carry the *l* of *fill* on to *a* and so get the effect of *filler* instead of *fill a*.[1]

We have already referred to Madame Sarah Bernhardt as an artist. I remember at the time of her death, one critic remarking, 'Oh, the crispness of her consonants!' A most important matter for all speakers as well as vocalists. On a certain occasion, the officiating priest in church was reading the New Testament. Amongst various incoherent sounds, I heard 'the se-of-the-fee,' which from the context I eventually found meant, 'the seed of the field.' The absence of the *d* rendered the sentence

[1] See *Science and Singing*, page 127.

unintelligible.[1] There is no doubt that a few people have the gift of a clear enunciation, but the majority have to work hard and

FIGURE 13.

I OFTEN LISTEN TO THY VOICE
BUT THY FACE I NEVER SEE!!

continually before this end is attained.[2] Still the result is worth the trouble, for the unmusical listener, as well as the musical, will enjoy a song if the words are distinct.

The vocal cord student is sometimes unfortunately subjected to a course of acrobatic jaw movements with the commendable object of inducing clarity of speech, but with results which are fatal to it. A professional gentleman holding a responsible position

[1] No wonder that Dr. Bell (Bishop of Chichester), in 1936 made a rule that in future all candidates for Holy Orders in his diocese must be proficient in voice production. They must show 'satisfactory evidence both of their ability to conduct the services of the church in such a way that the congregation can follow them intelligently, and also of their ability to read the Scriptures in a distinct and audible voice.' It is time that other bishops followed the lead.

[2] See *Science and Singing*, page 137.

at one of the important London musical colleges, came to me for lessons, in order to understand at first hand the various details of Sinus principles. He said to me at one of his early lessons, 'Mr. White, I find it so difficult to get freedom in pupils. They have such stiff jaws, I cannot get them to say *ah*'; and as he made the *ah* sound, he dropped his jaw with a big movement, leaving the mouth wide open. 'My dear sir,' I replied, 'my difficulty is to prevent pupils saying *ah*,' and I imitated his wide open mouth. But, he argued 'a pupil must learn to enunciate.' 'I agree,' I answered, 'but we do not enunciate with the jaw, we do so with our tongue, teeth and lips.' After due consideration, he was surprised to find that my statement was correct. A big jaw movement tends to prevent clear enunciation. Clarity of diction depends upon purity of vowel sounds, and strong 'crisp' consonants. The former is attained by a precise shaping of the mouth cavity but with little apparent movement, and the consonants should be made more emphatic in song than is usual in speech. Each of these can be accomplished with very little movement. So once again we see the importance of the 'principle of least action.'[1]

When this principle is thoroughly understood and carried out we shall not have such complaints as those of

A gentleman home from Malay
Who was taken one night to a play.
He said, 'I don't mind if their accent's refined,
But I wish I could hear what they say.'[2]

It is rather strange that singing and elocution tutors have not realized the lesson that can be learned from a good ventriloquist. Arthur Prince could fill the Coliseum with sound, and diction without a flaw, but even a movement of the mouth could hardly be detected. Of course it is granted that a vocalist need not be a ventriloquist, but a lesson can be learned from him.

A very good story, which I take by permission from *Time Was*, well shows the great care which must always be exercised, if clarity of diction in speech and song is to be ensured. The story runs as follows:

A sad example of first-night failure was his [Henry Irving's] long-contemplated and deeply studied *King Lear*. On the night of production he failed to make himself heard; he seemed to miss the pitch, his acting was superb, but his words inaudible.

[1] See *Science and Singing*, page 77*a*.

[2] Reproduced by kind permission of the proprietors of *Punch*.

At the end of the play he came before the curtain and made his usual short speech of thanks, each word falling clear cut as crystal from his lips and reaching the remotest corners of the theatre ; as he bowed and retired, a gentleman in the gallery called out, ' Why didn't yer speak like that before ? ' It voiced the feeling of the house, there was an unmistakable murmur of assent.

Irving came up to Ellen Terry, who had realized his failure and was greatly distressed. ' What did that man mean ? ' he asked, ' Have I not been speaking distinctly ? ' ' I couldn't hear a word you said from start to finish,' confessed Ellen, who knew that she would be cross-examined until she told the truth. ' Good God ! But—but why didn't you *tell* me ? ' ' Because you particularly asked me not to speak to you during the performance.'

And so it fell out that Irving's *Lear*, one of his most memorable impersonations, was recorded as a failure and will always be so remembered. It was a deep disappointment to him, all the more as he knew that his performance was good, nay of his very best.

So when a first-rate artist like Henry Irving can be caught nodding and off his guard in vocal technique during the whole evening's performance, it is not difficult to visualize the vigilance and care which the student vocalist must employ in order to keep a high standard of efficiency.

We must however bear in mind that a technical equipment, however complete, will never form an artist. There must be coupled with the technique a mental and psychological perception of musical art which is separate and distinct from acoustic laws and anatomy ; and so far as I can see this is more difficult to teach a pupil, because interpretation is not subject to law. Still, here again the determined student will make himself master of the whole situation. Nothing will escape his notice and zeal. What then can be said on the matter of pure artistry, without which technical rules will leave the soul unaffected ? It seems to me—although this is only a matter of opinion—that the sensation of fear is the cause of many failures. The vocalist wonders first of all whether she will succeed in getting her top note, or whether she will be able to make a good impression on the audience, or she may even fear lest the ladies recognize that she is wearing her last season's dress ! I confess I cannot offer a remedy for the last quandary, but for the other two the technique of Sinus principles gives an unfailing remedy, because the student has learned the control of his vocal machine and knows that the laws which he has learned theoretically and practically are permanent and will not let him down. Over and over again students have talked to me about being nervous. My reply has always been, 'You could not be so nervous that you would be unable to say what twice two make. Then know your work as thoroughly as you know your twice times table.'

'Knowledge is the antidote to fear,' wrote Emerson, and the Sinus student having a full knowledge of the technique of voice, and having thoroughly memorized both music and words, is able to concentrate his powers on appealing to his audience, and nervousness is the last detail to worry him. There is no room in his mind for any atmosphere of apprehension or anxiety while his work is actually in progress. Possibly a certain amount of excitement may be permitted to the artist as the day for the pending engagement draws near, but no trace of worry should ever dim his mind. A full command of the voice, however, must be the broom which will sweep away all trace of nerves.

Someone has said that 'fear is flight, with the body in chains.' Obviously flight under such conditions would be a failure, and the vocal artist who attempts to interpret his music in a state of fear has a very poor chance of success. I always try to impress my students with the idea that if they personally enjoy the music which they are giving to the audience then that feeling of enjoyment will be conveyed to those who are listening. It can hardly be expected that an audience will feel a spirit of enjoyment unless the artist can originate it. 'Dangers breed fears, and fears more dangers bring,'[1] but the Sinus trained artist fears no dangers, because he can always trust his vocal machine and knows every detail of his work. 'The fearless man is his own salvation.'[2]

Another very important asset for the singer is sincerity 'If I were asked,' writes Sydney Carroll, 'what quality the well graced actor can least afford to dispense with I should say "sincerity." My friend Mr. Godfrey Tearle is never tired of insisting upon the need for "the illusion of reality." No illusion is possible, no sense of realism is possible in the theatre unless the keynote of the player's work is that sovereign one of sincerity. It informs every line with truth. . . . The acid test of a player is found in that one word. Every sentence in the part must have sincerity underneath it, and behind it.' The advice is equally

[1] Pope.
[2] Robert Bridges.

important to the vocalist, because he also must frequently be an actor. Sir Charles Santley tells us in his book *Student and Singer*,[1] that he took the part of Elijah for the first time in Mendelssohn's oratorio for the Sacred Harmonic Society at Exeter Hall, early in March 1858. Being his first attempt it was not very successful. The work was repeated a week later, and as he left the platform at the close of the performance, Charles Lucas[2] came to him and patting him on the back said, ' You were Elijah to-night, my boy.'

A well-known writer[3] used to speak of ' the potency of attitude,' and the phrase is full of meaning for the vocalist. His mental ' attitude ' is the satisfactory assurance that he knows inside out, and if necessary upside down, the musical composition he is about to render; and further he has the immense joy of knowing that his vocal machine is equal to all the demands he will make on it. He is then free to give from his heart to the hearts of his audience all the spiritual meaning of the composition, feeling certain that ' only that which comes from the heart will appeal to the heart.' The art of Sinus Tone Production will relieve him from all technical anxiety, but the presentation of the words as a really living poem is quite a separate achievement and one that demands a personal transformation. The singer must stand before his audience and create a portrait of someone other than himself, with the emotions as expressed in the verse. The true artist must be constructive in the libretto as well as reproductive in the music. It has been said of painting, ' To transfer to canvas the thrust of the mind and soul, that is the supreme merit of all.'. This should also be the aim of the vocal artist, so to interpret both the music and the poem that those who are listening feel ' the thrust of the mind and soul.' Here, I believe, are described the various factors which go to make a successful vocalist.

It might be wise to add that consideration is required in making up a programme, whether it be for a complete recital or to fit in items in a general concert. For the sake of one's own credit it is important to avoid cheap trashy music, but on the other hand it is very risky to put on the programme, what for want of a better name is called ' highbrow ' music, by which we mean music which must be heard six or seven times before the listener is able

[1] Published by Edward Arnold & Co.,
[2] Principal of the Royal Academy of Music, 1859–1866.
[3] Edward Thring.

to discover what was in the mind of the composer. It is of course a matter of common knowledge that there is a very big selection of excellent German songs from which the concert artist can make his choice, but I would emphasize the further fact that if the vocalist will take the trouble, he can find many exquisite English and American songs which deserve far greater recognition than they have received.

We have spoken of the importance of 'sincerity' in the make-up of the artist, and a word might be added on the gift of imagination. Sir Rider Haggard said that he 'believed that imagination might even be a voice from Heaven whispering to our souls and enabling us to bring pleasure, and comfort, and joy, and help to others.' Here indeed is something which is worth the trouble, to bring 'comfort and joy and help to others.' But let the ambitious student be again reminded that the foundation of the whole big subject is a sound and dependable technique. Without this the spiritual superstructure can never be reared. 'Imagination' implies that it will be wise for the student to study the renderings given by artists of repute to any music which may be new in his vocal repertory, but that on no account should he feel that he must give the same or even a similar interpretation. My own custom is to make suggestions to pupils concerning the rendering of any song which is being studied, and then ask them to study the work and try to discover an alternative rendering which is as good or better. The matter is then discussed at the next lesson. In most cases the pupil will be well advised to accept the counsel of the tutor, for as Emma Calvé writes, 'Musical judgment, vocal understanding, is only gained by long practice and hard work. It cannot be acquired off-hand by any short cuts to success.' This was written with reference to vocal cord teaching, but its importance is much greater when applied to Sinus methods, because here the tutor has greater responsibilities inasmuch as it is his duty and special work to lay his finger on all weak vocal spots and to provide a satisfactory remedy. The Sinus tutor has such a full understanding of the pupil's vocal machine and its capabilities, that he will feel the responsibility of developing both beauty and power in every voice that is entrusted to his care. Obviously every voice is not capable of the same brilliancy, but every voice shall be trained through the tutor's power to its fullest competency. But when it comes to the interpretation of a song, though the tutor can advise, it is the student's imagination and sincerity which must bear the ultimate responsibility.

In the *Life of Jean de Reszke* by Clara Leiser,[1] the author writes that 'this studying, this searching for the way to achieve his artistic ideals, was done with very little help from teachers.' It is admitted by Clara Leiser that 'Jean de Reszke's teaching has been criticized by some of those who studied with him, as well as by others who did not. . . . He has also been criticized for not producing great singers from among his pupils.' From my own experience I know that his own pupils have adversely criticized his lessons, and it is quite certain that such directions as those mentioned on page 15*b* will not meet with the approval of those students who approve of Sinus methods. As an artist, however, he must have been superlative. After seeing him in opera, Jules Massenet wrote to him, 'You are unique in the rôle of Rodrigue, and you have a sincerity which no other will equal—it seems that you are really Rodrigue and Jean de Reszke at the same time.' Let it not however be imagined that brilliant success just rolled into his hands. He was invariably at the opera house two hours before the rising of the curtain, so that he could be sure of every detail in his make-up and get right into the spirit of his part. So must all artists concentrate, and they will not feel the doing so a hardship if they have their hearts genuinely in their work. Should this standard appear too high, then the choice of some other calling should be made. The career of a musical artist should be looked upon as a lofty one, for 'the language of music begins where the language of speech ceases.'[2] So in *The Dream of Gerontius*, whether you are a vocal soloist, a member of the chorus, or one of the orchestra with the second violins, you are assisting to bring to an audience the deep religious sentiment contained in the words and music of that oratorio. If your form of art consists in the presentation of humorous matter, there is still a high ideal to be carried out in making sad folk happy, if only for a few minutes. Sir Harry Lauder is very proud of his ability to provoke mirth—and rightly so. It is true that our achievement rarely reaches the mark of our endeavour, but that is not a very serious matter, for the ideal of the artist in its purity and beauty should always transcend the results produced.

[1] Published by Gerald Howe.
[2] Richard Wagner.

Many years ago I was at a public function sitting next to Sir John Bennett, the famous watchmaker, and he said to me, ' Had I been a shoe-black, I should never have rested until I was the best shoe-black in England.' Even so Ibsen has taught us, ' to care intensely for our work, to make it as good as we possibly could, without regard to the reward, to find pleasure in the pursuit, and to be content with the sympathy and understanding of a little clan.'[1]

1 Arthur Waugh.

CHAPTER VI

CONCLUSION

The hardest thing in the world, Sir, is to get possession of a fact—DR. SAMUEL JOHNSON.

IN *Rachmaninoff's Recollections*[1] the Russian composer, towards the end of the book, tells us : 'To-day, when the greater part of my life is over, I am constantly troubled by the misgiving that in venturing into too many fields, I have failed to make the best use of my life. In the old Russian phrase, "I have hunted three hares." Can I be sure that I have killed one of them ?' The three hares to which Sergei Rachmaninoff alluded, were his attempts to be conductor, pianist and composer. At the age of thirty he had not definitely decided to which section of music he should strenuously apply himself.

At the same age of thirty I had only just started the serious study of vocal problems, and was quite unconscious of the long years of endeavour which were in front of me, years which included a long struggle to develop into a good vocalist, ending in a dismal failure, loss of voice, and many months of medical attention. Eventually came the decision to pursue one 'hare,' to clear up the mystery which surrounded voice ; and that 'hare' has been relentlessly pursued for over forty years. Has the hare been killed ? Perhaps not killed, but it is getting winded and is running very lame. As a matter of fact, the 'hare' was found to have so many influential friends who were keen to preserve it from prying eyes and inquisitive watchers that it was found very difficult to circumscribe its course. I am however confident that notwithstanding its many friends who have done their utmost to protect it, the harmful and destructive career of this particular hare has now been so obstructed that its ultimate decease cannot be long delayed.

In *The Head Voice and Other Problems* it was acknowledged that 'the action of the vocal cords is but the first part of the unscientific controversy. What takes place above the vocal cords is equally mystifying. The offices of the pharynx, the mouth, the

[1] *Rachmaninoff's Recollections, told to Oskar von Riesemann.* Published by Allen & Unwin, Ltd.

nasal cavities, the entire structure of the head in fact, are rich in uncertainties.' This ' richness in uncertainties ' has been the field of operation for Sinus theories and practice, wherein, by scientific sifting and watchful analysis carried on by most careful consideration, the separation of truth from ' falsehood well disguised ' has been carried out, and a thoroughly reliable method of voice production has been achieved, to the benefit of both health and music. It may be true that ' from the first page of history to the last, the evidence abounds that people in high places cannot be trusted to behave with the discretion of men of ordinary competence ' ; yet even so, one might have reasonably imagined that many years of brilliant success would have caused one or two of the ' people in high places ' to meditate and consider which is preferable, the Tolstoyan gloom which envelops the vocal cord theories of voice, admittedly ' mysterious,' ' chaotic,' and void of scientific foundation, or alternatively, the tenets of Sinus theories which are, in Stevenson's phrase, radiantly simple ! ' *A little child shall lead them.*' Small choir-boys and children in elementary schools can understand and put into practice Sinus theories and revel in the freedom of singing and beauty of tone, whilst our academies and those who control them refuse to move. ' We are all more or less riveted to the present,' writes Prof. Charles Richet, and apparently our musical and medical dons have neither wish nor intention of moving from the 1,700-year-old theory that voice is produced at the vocal cords. It must be because, as Bacon put it, ' Truth comes out of error much more rapidly than it comes out of confusion,' or because, in Ernest Newman's words, ' A good lie, once it gets a start, can never be caught up with.'

It has been well said that the ' one great criterion of science is the test of utility.'[1] When a key is offered for use, ' I am not,' as Sir Arthur Eddington has expressed it, ' among those who are turning it over and over, unable to decide from the look of it whether it is good metal or base metal. The question for me is, will it unlock the door ? ' That is the test which has for nearly forty years been applied again and again to Sinus theories and each time the door of difficulty has been unlocked, and so once again we see ' the long accepted truth to be merely long accepted error.'[2]

[1] Rev. T. Wigley, M.A.
[2] Ernest Newman.

'The assertion that outstrips the evidence,' Huxley once said, 'is not only a blunder but a crime.' On which side lies the weight of evidence, for or against Sinus theories? If antiquity be accepted as evidence of truth, we start with a heavy weight against Sinus principles; but antiquity is of very little value as evidence. In fact, for the consideration of vocal matters the antiquity of vocal cord theories should count against their being accepted as truth, for after hundreds of years of vocal cord study, its exponents are unable to agree upon any precise and recognized method of training. This cannot be due to lack of opportunity. But even the few points of agreement which are accepted are so vague as to fail in the test of utility. Surely long experience should have produced something better for the assistance of the student than inappropriate metaphors. Such directions do not explain what are the rules of the game. 'A law,' to quote G. K. Chesterton, 'is something that can be broken,' but in the case of the vocal cord tutor's vague directions, 'one can neither have the firmness of keeping laws, or the fun of breaking them.' Here we have the reason why such eminently clever people as Sir Henry Wood, Sir Percy Buck, the late Dr. Mann, and Viola Tree, besides thousands of others, were never able to sing satisfactorily. The delectable bees (mentioned on page 14*a*) have left their mark and we recognize the result of their work.

'What is the supposed disadvantage of Sinus principles?[1] I cannot remember that any disadvantage has ever been pointed out. . . . Apart from our reluctance to tackle a difficult and unfamiliar conception' of voice, the whole evidence of truth is on the side of the new vocal theory. The late Sir Arthur Thomson declared that 'the sciences are most scientific when they are most united,' and it is the complete unison which is shown in these pages between design and function, voice and health,[2] which gives the lie to the ancient vocal cord tradition and fixes the seal of truth on its successor. 'Nature's has been a stern school,' says the same author, 'she has let no slackness go unpunished. . . . Nature is all for health.' Because they have not known the importance of clean, well ventilated sinuses, Nature has afflicted mankind with bronchitis, deafness, consumption, pyorrhea, and numerous other ills.

[1] Again I am indebted to Eddington for this phraseology. In his book *The Expanding Universe*, he asks the question concerning curved space; I alter the words 'curved space' and substitute 'Sinus principles.'

[2] See pages 61-4.

'Keats could not forgive Newton for robbing mankind of the wonder of the rainbow, but when minor mysteries disappear, greater mysteries stand confessed. Science never destroys wonder, but only shifts it higher and deeper.'[1] My professional brethren I know are vexed with me for having robbed them of the mysteries which for centuries have surrounded the vocal cords, and permitted the writing of rubbish which no pen but that of a singing tutor would put on paper. The serious student of Sinus work will realize how very much 'higher and deeper' are the real wonders of throat and head, which unfold as anatomy and acoustics are found to harmonize in a truly wonderful way. In a splendid book by Logan Clendening, *Behind the Doctor*,[2] the following passage occurs:

> Clever fellow that doctor. How did he know all that? How did he know so well what to do? Must have learned it from somebody—medical school or something—but where did they learn it? Medical school teachers had to learn it too!
>
> Who's behind the doctor? Behind the doctor—so many centuries, so many stories, so many people, I see them crowding around him—a great throng of old ghosts as he walks into the room. When he takes out his stethoscope to listen to your heart, there is thin, consumptive Dr. Laennec, of Paris, peering over his shoulder. When he taps your chest, another ghost—jolly, music-loving Dr. Leopold Auenbrugger, of Vienna—smiles in appreciation of his discovery living through the years. As your doctor dresses those stitches, I see little, old Ambroise Paré, and gentle Joseph Lister behind him. Near your anaesthesia apparatus is the ghost of poor Horace Wells, who cut his radial artery from disappointment and bled to death. Many other ghosts, too! Interesting, queer people. William Harvey, the Englishman, sitting on the benches of the old anatomical theatre at Padua; and Andreas Vesalius, the Belgian, slinking through the dusky streets of Paris with a skeleton in his wheelbarrow. All these and thousands of others are behind the doctor. Vivid people in their day, full of hope and interests and queer notions.

Yes, such 'queer notions' were these new ideas to those who first came across them, that each originator of each 'queer notion' had to fight desperately for the new truth before it was received and adopted. 'Hard are the ways of truth and rough to walk,' wrote Milton. 'Such is the law which God has annexed to the promulgation of the truth; its preachers suffer, but its

[1] Sir Arthur Thomson.

[2] Published by Wm. Heinemann & Sons, Ltd.

cause prevails,' wrote Cardinal Newman. And who can we say is ' behind ' the vocal tutor of to-day ? Practically there is no one. The physician Galen in the second century attributed voice to vocal cord action and there it has remained ever since. Porpora and his contemporaries in the early eighteenth century have the credit of training some excellent voices, but how far that credit is deserved we are unable to tell. No doubt there were vocal geniuses in the eighteenth century, as there have been in the nineteenth and twentieth, and it has needed very little skill to train them. Quite naturally history does not relate how many failures there were under the much-talked-of ' Old Italian method,' but we do know that no trace of any definite teaching system has ever been found whereby we could work out a scientific course of vocal training. Inasmuch as the anatomical knowledge of these people was exceedingly limited,[1] it is very doubtful if they had the foundation on which any precise form of voice training could be based.

As late as the early years of the nineteenth century, so difficult was it for students to gain a knowledge of human anatomy that they had to do it surreptitiously, and villains used to thrive by strangling victims and selling their bodies to the surgeons. Ghouls followed funerals at a distance, and waiting until darkness fell, would dig up the new interred bodies and sell them to the hospitals. ' Resurrectionists ' they were called.[2]

That being the state of things in the nineteenth century, we cannot imagine that the vocal tutors a hundred years earlier were better informed. Thus it was clearly impossible for Porpora and his associates to give any definite teaching based on anatomical or scientific knowledge. The name of Manuel Garcia (1805–1906) will always live as the inventor of the laryngoscope, but that little instrument has never helped anyone to control the voice, or to move a hair's breadth towards improving it. ' Behind ' the vocal tutor of to-day working on orthodox lines there is not a single person on whose work we can scientifically build.

' I don't think much of the man who is not wiser to-day than he was yesterday,' said Abraham Lincoln, but our vocal tutors to-day actually pride themselves on basing their training on the traditional precepts of men whose knowledge must from the nature

1 See Figure 1.
2 *The Conquest of Disease.* See Appendix XII.

of things have been shallow in the extreme. Obviously there can be no stigma on their personal character, or on their work, for this ignorance, but rather their successes are to be so much the more admired. The matter for astonishment is that present-day musical colleges, notwithstanding the many failures which abound in their studios, and the many successes which are accredited to the Sinus system, refuse even to consider a fresh thought on their vocal work. Or rather, it would be a matter for astonishment, did we not realize in the light of history, that this is just the kind of reception which must be expected by any original thinker or worker.

I have had many enthusiasts for my work and many against it. The former I regard with joy and pleasure, the latter with a kind of sympathy, as when a certain person was looking at a Turner water-colour over which an enthusiast was waxing eloquent with delight: the uninitiated one coldly remarked that he 'could see nothing in it.' 'No,' came the ready reply, 'do you not wish you could?' Some people have remarked to me, 'I like your book and theories, but cannot go the whole way with you.' 'This,' I reply, 'is an impossible attitude.' The vocal cords either create tone or they do not. If they do, then *Science and Singing* is an abominable book fit only for the fire; otherwise the volume contains a very wonderful truth which will astonish the world, not only by its freshness, but by the practical results which follow the theory. To my mind, an intermediate position is logically impossible, the two ideas cannot possibly mix. 'Truth and falsehood . . . are like the iron and clay in the toes of Nebuchadnezzar's image, they may cleave, but they will not incorporate.'[1] The truth of Sinus Tone Production is not likely to lack appreciation, for the idea has spread over the world, and too many people have now had practical experience of its value, to allow it to disappear into oblivion, but so far as any public recognition of forty years of research is concerned, I have to be satisfied with Emerson's assurance: 'The reward of a thing well done is to have done it.' 'The larger the dream the heavier the price,' wrote Arthur Waugh. My dream—the creation of a scientific system of voice control and production for the whole world—was surely a large one. The price I have paid has been heavy: sleepless nights, self-denial from amusements and recreation, expense for books and other

[1] Bacon.

publications. The world has not yet been conquered. Orthodoxy holds too strong and unbending a position to allow this. Mr. Kaikhosru Shapurji Sorabji, writing in the *New English Weekly*, says :[1]

> Like all discoverers and pioneers Mr. White has had a full share of misrepresentation, abuse and ridicule from the upholders of the vested interests of orthodox views . . . who refuse even to envisage, let alone admit, the possibility of salvation outside their own pet system, even, or one should rather say, particularly, when all their own best—or worst—efforts have ignominiously failed, and those of unorthodoxy have proved brilliantly successful with those very failures. . . . On almost every page of Mr. White's books is something so utterly destructive—to an unbiassed reader—of the orthodox teachings, that it is a matter for amazement that the older theories can still obtain any sort of credence.

To obtain a whole-hearted judgment of this character is in itself no small reward. Add to this the fact that we have in existence a Guild of the Voice Beautiful, with over 200 members, formed for the purpose of making known those benefits alluded to in the *New English Weekly*, and it will be seen that even though the world of music, science and medicine has not yet seen fit to acknowledge the supremacy of Sinus Tone Production, yet an excellent and worthy start has been made in proving that an advance has been made upon the hoary, antiquated, contradictory ideas of vocal cord tone emission. ' If I were ambitious,' wrote Havelock Ellis, ' I would desire no finer epitaph than that it should be said of me, " He has added a little to the sweetness of the world and a little to its light." ' The results of Sinus theories show that the work has succeeded in each of these respects. In the language of the mathematicians, it is ' common to both.'

Galileo gave us the epigrammatic phrase, ' The Bible teaches us how to go to Heaven. It does not teach how the heavens go.' The art of Sinus Tone Production teaches the vocal student ' how ' the voice ' goes,' and thus he is able to direct his course to his desired heaven, namely, the power of creating beautiful vocal tone. This the vocal cord theory of voice has never been able to effect, but states that a voice is either ' worth training ' or it is ' not worth training.' The Sinus tutor recognizes no such condition. *Every* voice is worth training, as every soul is worth saving. So far as I am concerned, this will be the final volume on

[1] In the issue of 17th January 1935.

the subject from my pen. No doubt books on vocal problems will continue to flow from the press; but I am convinced that after nearly forty years of careful and concentrated research, it is now time that I put *finis* to this part of my work. I can do so with satisfaction and peace of mind knowing that 'I have fought a good fight,' and believing that 'the sweetest canticle when a man hath obtained worthy ends and expectations is *Nunc Dimittis*.'

NOTE

This being the last volume which is likely to appear from the pen of the author, he desires to put on record here the debt of gratitude which he feels that he owes to those friends who through years of persistent endeavour have never failed to cheer and encourage him in the difficult and sometimes painful experiences which beset the path of the pioneer. To all these he offers now his very sincere and most grateful thanks. The names are not placed in any order of merit, but approximately in the order in which they became acquainted with Sinus principles of voice. Should any names unfortunately be omitted, it is hoped that those friends will be generous and realize that the oversight was unintentional.

Miss Mildred Day, Rother Dene, Sheet, near Petersfield, Hants.

The late George F. Barwick, Esq., B.A., Keeper of Printed Books at the British Museum.

The late Mrs. Wightwick.

Reginald F. Price, Esq., M.D., C.M., 58 Sebert Road, Forest Gate, London, E.7.

Mrs. R. Price, 58 Sebert Road, Forest Gate, London, E.7.

W. H. Chisholm, Esq., 9 Camomile Street, E.C.3, and Restharrow, Hartley, Longfield, Kent.

Dom Alphege Shebbeare, O.S.B., The Presbytery, Callow End, Worcester.

The Right Reverend Adrian Taylor, O.S.B., M.A., M.C., Abbot of Ramsgate.

The Very Rev. Canon Pritchard, Priest's House, Hazlewell Road, Putney, S.W.15.

A. D. Hewlett, Esq., B.Litt., M.A., Abbotsholme School, Derby.

Dom Bernard McElligott, O.S.B., M.A., Ampleforth Abbey, York.

J. Gilbert Curtis, Esq., Organist and Choir Director of Christ Church, Willaston, Cheshire.

Ronald Dussek, Esq., F.R.C.O., Precentor, Radley College, Abingdon, Berks.

Miss Mary Deane, The Lodge, Radley College, Abingdon, Berks.

The Right Reverend Adrian Taylor, O.S.B., M.A., M.C., Abbot of Ramsgate.

David S. Spence, Esq., M.B., The Mental Hospital, Wells, Somerset.

A. W. Fitzsimmons, Esq., 13 Chichester Rents, Chancery Lane, London, W.C.2.

Christopher Davis, Esq., Organist and Choirmaster of St. Simon Stock, Putney.

Douglas Stevens, Esq., L.R.A.M., A.L.A.M., 47 Graham Road, Purley, Surrey.

James E. Brydone, Esq., 26 Meadowside, Cambridge Park, Twickenham, Middlesex.

Miss Elizabeth A. M. Stratton, 13 Camberwell Terrace, Antrim Road, Belfast.

David J. Rayner, Esq., 28 Weigall Road, Lee, London, S.E.12

Herbert G. Taylor, Esq., 47 Polwarth Gardens, Edinburgh.

Dom Gregory Murray, O.S.B., M.A., F.R.C.O., Downside Abbey, Bath, Somerset.

Rev. Sylvester Fryer, O.S.B., Ampleforth Abbey, York.

Miss Audrey Hodgson, L.R.A.M., A.R.C.M., L.G.S.M., 52 Montgomery Road, Sheffield.

APPENDICES

APPENDICES

I, PAGE 4

In his book *The Science and Sensations of Vocal Tone*, Mr. E. Herbert-Caesari tells us that 'the *lower* the note the *thicker*, *longer* and *looser* the vocal cords,' and places lines within an isosceles triangle to illustrate this point. The idea is certainly ingenious and is what one may expect if the vocal cords produce tone. Unfortunately, however, for the author's theory, it requires but little argument to show that it is incorrect. As a cord gets longer, it cannot possibly get thicker and looser, but on the contrary gets thinner and tighter ! Conversely he informs his readers that the *higher* the note, the *thinner*, *shorter* and *lighter* the vocal cords. Here again one does not shorten an elastic cord and expect it to get lighter and thinner. I am quite aware that the vocal cord enthusiast will argue that we are not dealing with ordinary cords, but with vocal cords. In that case he will place himself in the unsound and dangerous position of asserting that the vocal cords act in direct opposition to universal laws and so run counter to the fundamental postulate of science which is the uniformity of nature. We shall presently see that the conforming to this fundamental postulate is one of the many strong points which uphold Sinus theories.

II, PAGE 15

Two of the subjects for discussion at the conference referred to in the text, were on the agenda as follows : (*a*) 'Are the present methods of teaching singing an improvement on those of the Old Italian Masters ? ' (*b*) 'To what extent uniformity of method is possible or desirable ? ' The former was quickly settled by the very apt criticism of Mr. Steuart Wilson, who remarked, 'No one knows what *bel canto* really was, not even Herman Klein could tell us that.' Those who have read *Light on the Voice Beautiful* will know in what an amusing manner Mr. Wilson's statement is there verified.[1] Section (*b*) was less successful. Mr. Ronald Dussek[2] suggested that it was advisable to have uniformity of method in teaching. This drew from the chairman for the evening the question, 'What method would you suggest ? ' and Mr. Dussek replied, 'Sinus Tone Production.' Mr. Steuart Wilson was most emphatic in supplying a vigorous negative to this proposal. 'Do we,' said he, 'want only

[1] See pages 172 and 173.
[2] Precentor of Radley College.

one kind of religion, do we want only one kind of architecture, do we want only one school of painting ?' The late Mr. Plunket Greene was energetic in supporting this line of thought and, of course, the whole meeting with such a lead fell into line and agreement. Although I was present at the meeting, I felt it would be inopportune to attempt a pitched battle on the subject. It would, however, have been easy to show the weakness and instability of Mr. Wilson's argument. It is, of course, quite clear that we do not wish to have only one style of painting. J. M. W. Turner probably would not have even wished to create scenes such as those beloved by Farquharson, and neither artist would have had interest in depicting the scenes chosen by R. Caton Woodville ; but varied as were the subjects and styles of these men, yet each had to carry out fundamental principles of balance, light and shade, and perspective, for their art work. Similarly, laws of proportion and strain must be observed by the architect whether he is designing a cottage or a palace. As regards religion would Mr. Wilson have us believe that all religions are of equal value ? If so there can be no need for the Church Missionary Society, the Society for the Propagation of the Gospel, and other societies. The Christian religion has undoubtedly shades of thought containing important variations, but the fundamental creed is the same, although it allows differences. Such was the meaning in the mind of Mr. Dussek when he suggested that Sinus Tone Production should be the basis of vocal training, because in that system, well defined acoustic laws are made the basis of all work, which certainly cannot be claimed for vocal cord tuition.

III, PAGE 18

What is the cause of the undoubted success which has attended the teachings of the Matthay School of pianoforte playing ? It is the fact that Mr. Tobias Matthay reduced—or shall we say advanced—the teaching of pianoforte playing to a mechanical system. I have heard people deny the credit of this originality to Mr. Matthay, and I am not in a position to discuss the point, but I do know, and positively affirm, that I personally learned more in a lesson of one hour from Mr. York Bowen—one of Mr. Matthay's most prominent pupils, than I previously learned in years of training at the—— School of Music, and elsewhere. Mr. Matthay wisely realized that many people have the artistic soul, and the ' mental concept ' of glorious music, but lack the mechanical control and efficiency to produce it. What scales fell from my eyes when I was taught how to act, or, as Mr. F. Matthias Alexander would say, to understand ' the means whereby ' I could produce an even scale of legato or staccato notes ! Commenting on that wonderful violin tutor Otakar Sevcik, the *Daily Telegraph* remarks, ' This man who had produced more skilled technicians than any other teacher of his time, ascribed his success solely to patience, perseverance and *method*. His immense labours in reducing every technical combination possible on the violin to a system, seemed to him nothing more than the carrying of an accepted principle of technique to its logical conclusion.' This is precisely the work carried out for voice by Sinus principles. They give a scientific and controllable technique where none previously existed.

The late Dame Clara Butt a little time since in an interview remarked, 'Considering how many English people attempt to sing, it is a little surprising that we do not produce more truly great professionals. But the fact is, a notion of good elementary technics is rare. There are probably singers among our choirs and amateur soloists who have possibilities of real eminence, but who will never be pleasing to hear—they sing on wrong lines and do not know how to right themselves. . . . The teaching of singing is in a chaotic state.' Dame Clara Butt studied for years at the Royal College of Music and also abroad, so her opinion is valuable. Furthermore, it is correct, for those singers who are unsatisfactory or perhaps bad, fail chiefly for want of definite and scientific instruction.

IV, PAGE 18

'A tone is not a thing to see, and the teacher cannot use a camera and a manometric flame in teaching tone production.' Here there is that infinitely dangerous thing, a half truth. We, of course, go to a concert to hear the music and not to see it, as we go to a picture gallery in order to see the pictures and not hear them. That, however, is but a small part of the argument. The marvellous tone and variety of tones which Kreisler can produce with his violin, is surely the *result* of an extraordinary technique, whose mechanism can be explained in mechanical terms and can be laid open to the vision although the results of the technique can be heard and not seen.

V, PAGE 25

There have been other attempts to produce an alternative theory of voice production, for example by Mr. J. van Brockhoven and Monsieur Léon Lievens. The vocal theory of the first named author is considered in *Science and Singing*, so needs no further notice here. The French writer has, in red capital letters on the title page of his book, *La Vérité Vocale sur la Voix Humaine*, 'JAMAIS, LE LARYNX N'A ETE L'ORGANE DE LA VOIX. JAMAIS, L'HOMME N'A EU DE CORDES VOCALES.' His idea of voice is that the diaphragm pushes the air from the lungs, through the vocal cords into the maxillary sinus and so produces sound in that cavity. This would appear to be a more likely theory of voice than vocal cord sonority, for there is a large hollow chamber where it is conceivable that tonal vibrations might be formed. But one can hardly expect one chamber to be responsible for two octaves of human voice. Other difficulties in the matter are that the acceptance of the theory would necessitate an upward pressure of air including energetic activity of the diaphragm and the further serious disadvantage that we are unable to exercise a personal control over the maxillary sinus.

FIGURE 14. SPIRAL BUNDLE OF HOP STEMS

VI, PAGE 42

Dr. Pettigrew's work seemed to me so extraordinarily instructive that I have secured his permission to reprint the following further passages, with some of his figures.

While the vast system of spiral nebulae, spiral cyclones, spiral sand storms, spiral water spouts, whirlpools, etc., are on a scale of unexampled magnificence and splendour, there yet exist microscopic spiral arrangements in great plenty which are quite as interesting in a way to the chemist and physiologist, as the others are to the astronomer and physicist. Examples of the minute spirals are to be found in crystals, plants and animals, especially in the latter.

The organic spirals abound in plants and animals, but all of them, whether organic or inorganic, bear a resemblance to each other, showing a common origin and a community of function. Spiral tendrils, in some respects, resemble hands and feet and climbing plants generally possess the latent property of limbs. . . . In the higher animals walking, swimming and flying are all performed by the aid of distinctly spiral organs ; the bones of the bodies and limbs being twisted upon themselves in a variety of ways. . . . The great importance of spirals in the inorganic and organic kingdoms can scarcely be exaggerated.

Figure 14 shows a spiral bundle of hop stems. The stems twine into each other and form left-handed spirals. Figure 15 shows spiral stems and tendrils of the passion flower.

Examples of spiral arrangements in man are well shown in Figures 16, 17 and 18.

Continued on page 131.

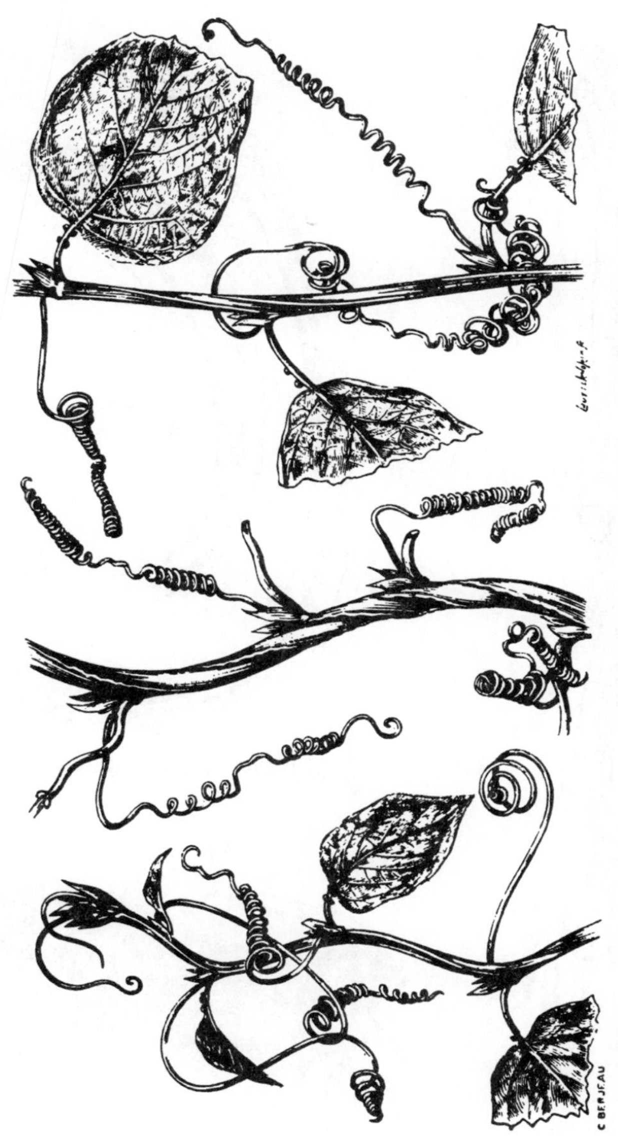

FIGURE 15. SPIRAL STEMS AND TENDRILS OF THE PASSION FLOWER

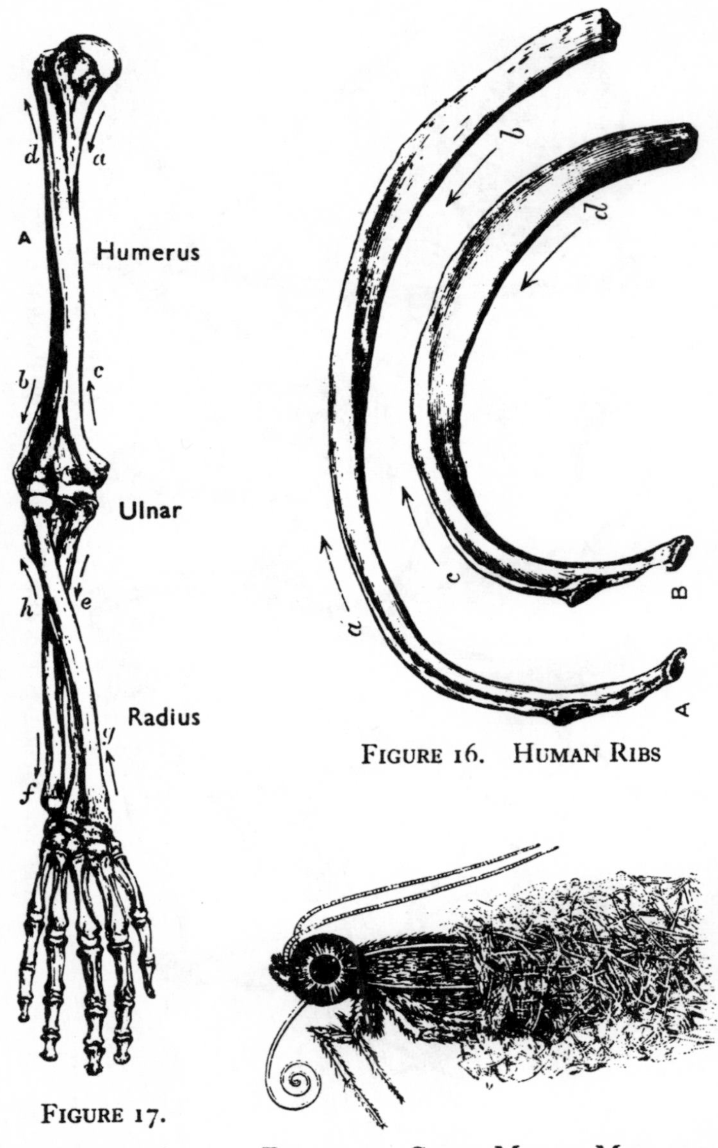

FIGURE 16. HUMAN RIBS

FIGURE 17.
THE HUMAN ARM

FIGURE 19. CLOTH MOTH. MAGNIFIED

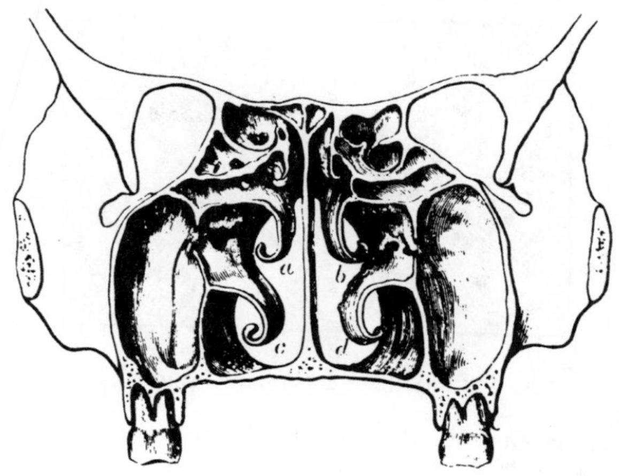

FIGURE 18.
TRANSVERSE SECTION OF TURBINATED BONES
IN THE HUMAN SKULL

Figure 16 shows human ribs not only spiral in shape but also twisted upon themselves. It will be noted that Figure 18 is very similar to Figure 4 in *Science and Singing*. That in *Science and Singing* gives a clearer idea of the relative positions of nose, mouth and eyes, but Figure 18 gives the curves of the bones in clearer detail. The curved bones *c* and *d* are the inferior turbinated bones, and *a* and *b* are the middle turbinated bones. Compare Figure 3, *H*, *N*, in *Science and Singing*, page 17. The straight bone in the centre is the septum of the nose corresponding to *Y*, Figure 2, in *Science and Singing*.

Figure 17 shows the upper arm (the humerus), the forearm (the ulnar and radius) and the hand.

To those versed in medical knowledge it is of course unnecessary to stress any details in the build and structure of these bones, but those who have not made a study of anatomy should note how the radius, the smaller of the two bones in the forearm, crosses the ulnar from *g* to *h*. The upper end at *h* is smaller than the lower end at *g* which carries the hand. It should be noted that the humerus of the upper arm curves on itself from *a* to *b* and from *c* to *d*.

These illustrations are but a few out of hundreds which could be given. ‘The universality of the spiral in nature is a subject alike for surprise and reflection,’ writes Dr. Pettigrew in his second volume. The universality of it was indeed to me a matter of surprise. How many people are there who would imagine that the ordinary cloth moth has a spiral proboscis such as this? (Figure 19.)

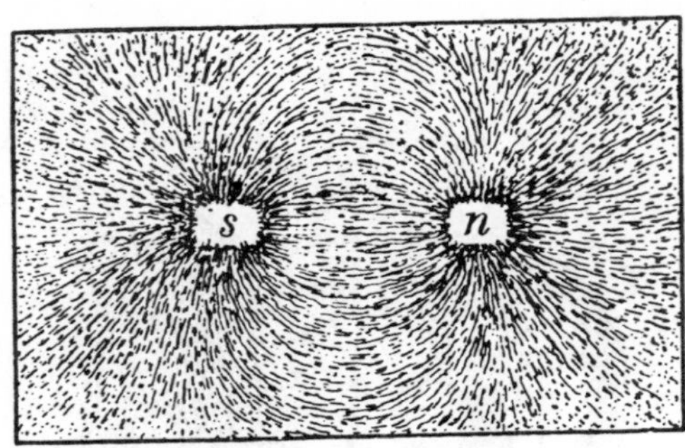

FIGURE 20. LINES OF FORCE

Figure 20, taken from Professor H. Ebert's work *Magnetic Fields of Force*, shows the lines of force.

VII, PAGE 52

An interesting side-light on this anatomical structure is to be seen in the fixing of a kitchen stove of the 'Ideal' type. The manufacturers direct that 'the flue outlet of the stove must be tight sealed at the place where it enters the chimney. Unless this is done the draught may be spoiled by the cold air entering the chimney and the stove will not do its work.'

How similar this is to the actions of the soft palate and uvula. The air column coming up direct from the lungs would probably be at a higher temperature than that in the mouth, and it certainly would be of a different chemical composition.[1] It is, therefore, a matter of importance that the air column which is on its way to the creation of tone should be free from all interference from the air which is in the mouth.

Once again, in two completely different matters, we see 'the uniformity of nature.'

Mr. Charles Holden, the architect who designed the premises of the British Medical Association and the University of London, was in 1936 presented, at a meeting of the Royal Institute of British Architects, with the Royal Gold Medal awarded by the King. On this occasion he remarked, 'Is there anything more beautiful than the healthy human body, and anything in nature or art which shows a more complete economy in design?' Yet the only design which our vocal tutors have found in the graceful lines of the soft palate and uvula is one which will destroy their utility.

[1] See *Science and Singing*, page 71.

VIII, PAGE 59

In the Royal Library at Windsor are nearly six hundred anatomical drawings by that wonderful artist Leonardo da Vinci (1452-1519). These have been reproduced in miniature by Kenneth Clarke[1] and published by the Cambridge University Press. Not one of all these drawings shows the frontal or sphenoid sinuses, nor the ethmoid cells, so that one might well suppose that at the beginning of the sixteenth century their existence was unknown. One drawing gives the maxillary sinus with the orbital cavity.

About 1906 I was paying many visits to the Museum of the Royal College of Surgeons at Lincoln's Inn and although in one room there were hundreds of skulls arranged in cases on the walls, neither the curator nor I could find even six skulls so cut that the size and disposition of the sinuses could be compared. Thus it is only very recently that this important part of our anatomy has had even the smallest consideration, and it is only now that the immense importance of bringing them into action is beginning to dawn on the medical profession.

IX, PAGE 62

I feel impelled to give one more case because it was undertaken by my pupil, Mr. Gilbert Curtis. A lady suffering from aphonia and experiencing great pain in attempting even a whisper was under treatment from her local doctor and a throat specialist from October 1936 to June 1937. At the end of that time the medical man informed his patient that he could do no more for her and the case must be regarded as hopeless. The same evening Mr. Curtis was called in, and after two hours' treatment on Sinus methods her voice returned and she has experienced no further trouble. Full particulars of this case may be had if desired.

X, PAGE 63

In my first book, *Science and Singing* (published 1909), I ventured to make the bold prophecy that in course of time the practice of Sinus Tone Production would gradually diminish the number of those people who were deaf and dumb until eventually the trouble ceased to exist.

My suggestion was misunderstood and brought sarcastic remarks from the medical press. Having now an opportunity I should like to express myself more clearly. The proper control of the head cavities was never understood until the art of Sinus Tone Production was evolved, nor is there, so far as I am aware, any medical work which even hints at the possibility of control. I can, therefore, claim to make the original statement that a very high percentage of

[1] Director of the National Gallery and Surveyor of the King's Pictures.

people never use their frontal sinuses at all, whilst a larger number, including children, confine the voice to the activity of the sphenoid sinus only. All, therefore, that I suggest is that the use or disuse of the sinuses will follow the same laws as other parts of the body. In vision it is necessary to make use of both eyes ; the organist should make full use of both feet, and the tennis player of both arms in order to get the best results. But should anyone allow one eye, one foot or hand to remain permanently inactive, its vitality will gradually disappear. Hence it seems to me a reasonable supposition that people who have for generations failed to use both frontal sinus and ethmoid cells should eventually degenerate to the point of being voiceless. I have never suggested that a child who is born with an incomplete auditory apparatus could be taught to hear and hence to speak by means of Sinus theories, but I have heard deaf mutes create sounds which I believe could be very considerably developed on Sinus lines.

During the 29 years which have elapsed since *Science and Singing* was published, Sinus theories have made considerable progress and their scope for good has enlarged. In consequence of these experiences, I now venture to propose another daring impression, namely, that the terrible curse of cancer may in some cases arise through the poisonous germs of infected sinuses. It will doubtless take some years to test the correctness of the speculation, but I believe the suggestion is full of possibilities. I must add that I do not expect that Sinus theories will act as a cure for cancer after the evil has started.

At the fourth annual meeting of the Guild of the Voice Beautiful, Dr. Reginald Price said that ' to-day greater stress was laid upon preventive research than curative and in his opinion it was in the former that the practical application of Sinus principles would prove to be invaluable.'

XI, PAGE 92

' Since E. G. White's work on Sinus Tone Production, there is no excuse for any voice specialist who does not recognize that the sole role of the vocal cords is to govern the supply of breath.' (Oliver C. de C. Ellis), *Daily Telegraph*, 29th May 1937.

XII, PAGE 117

In reference to resurrectionists it may be interesting to know that a ' watch-house ' is still preserved in the graveyard of All Hallows-the-Less, in Lower Thames Street, London. The church was destroyed in the Great Fire. The watch-house is adjacent to the licensed premises known as 'The Hour Glass. On the face of the relic the following inscription appears :

In the year 1557 this watch-house was erected to guard the graves from the unwelcome attention of the Resurrectionists. The exterior of this building remains exactly the same as it was when first built. At the pavement level you will see a small arched recess where the watchman kept his bell. In addition to guarding the graveyard of All Hallows-the-Less adjoining this watch-house, it was the watchman's duty to perambulate the neighbourhood at night and call on the citizens to put out their lights and fires.

There is also a watch tower in St. Sepulchre's Church, at the corner of Holborn Viaduct and Giltspur Street, immediately opposite St. Bartholomew's Hospital. Tradition holds that it was placed there to prevent students from the hospital doing a little ' resurrecting ' work in St. Sepulchre's churchyard when they were ' hard up.'

WARNING

In consequence of the continued success of the practical application of Sinus principles there are unfortunately many unqualified people who are now professing to teach the method. Whilst admitting that these people may produce some good results it is important to give a word of warning that with such tuition it is impossible to get the full benefits of the system. The art of Sinus Tone Production, like other scientific subjects, requires some years of training before such proficiency can be gained as will entitle the student to become a tutor. The author gave signed permission to act as such to those students who were trained by him and gave satisfactory proof of their understanding and ability to teach. A register is kept of all the names of authorized teachers and enquiries may be made from The Director of Studies, St. Monica, East Chinnock, Yeovil, Somerset.

INDEX OF NAMES

INDEX OF SUBJECT MATTER